# Introduction

HAVING PREPARED FOR publication the extraordinarily fraudulent document that is George Psalmanazar's *Historical and Geographical Description of Formosa*, it was an easy decision to do likewise with his Memoirs. Psalmanazar was a fascinating character, and these Memoirs, published intentionally on his instructions after his death in London in 1765, provide what might even be a truthful account of much of his life. But not all of it.

He was known primarily throughout his life for the scam he pulled in his early twenties, when he claimed to be born on the island of Formosa off the coast of China. This falsehood gained such traction and was so useful to him in terms of setting himself up in England that he started to embellish the story, and wrote a whole book, almost entirely out of his own imagination, describing the geography, history, culture and society of Formosa. He just made it all up, and managed to keep up the front through two successful editions of the book and several learned debates with some of the wisest and most knowledgeable men of his age. He also created at least the appearance of a fake language, both spoken and written. In the annals of charlatanry, Psalmanazar's Formosan Fraud has a special place.

After he was exposed, and to some extent admitted the ruse, he became a devout Christian, proclaiming his strong belief in the religion of "revelation", that people could and did have direct contact with God, personal experiences of the Divine. He also became a writer subsisting at the lower end of the London writing ladder, churning out words to be published in the books of others, in return for just enough to live on. He knew Samuel

Johnson and other literary luminaries, and would have been a celebrity of sorts, having created a massive and successful literary fraud, and lived to confess and move on to another identity.

His Memoirs, published in full here, are still readable, even though written nearly four hundred years ago in the verbose style of the day.

The memoir, he writes in his Will, is "a faithful narrative of my education, and the sallies of my wretched youthful years, and the various ways by which I was in some measure unavoidably led into the base and shameful imposture of passing upon the world for a native of Formosa, and a convert to Christianity, and backing it with a fictitious account of that island, and of my own travels, conversion, &c. all or most of it hatched in my own brain, without regard to truth and honesty."

Why did he only have it published posthumously? He says it was to make it more convincing, "less liable to suspicion, as the author would be far out of the influence of any sinister motives that might induce him to deviate from the truth."

He leaves his origins veiled in mystery. Even the name of the Memoirs does not give his real name, replaced with a series of four asterisks. But he was born probably in 1679 in southwestern France in relative poverty, and this book tells the story of how he escaped to the Western world's richest city, London, and became a star of the publishing and intellectual worlds. For a time.

In his Will, he expresses remorse for having foisted the Formosa fraud on the world: "I think myself bound to beg God and the world pardon for writing [it], and have been long since, as I am to this day, and shall be as long as I live, heartily sorry for, and ashamed of." He talks of "the great load of guilt" he bore in all the decades that followed the exposure of the forgery. And maybe he did, who knows. And yet, No matter how it is viewed, his life almost certainly played out better than it would

# MEMOIRS OF
## ＊＊＊＊

---

## The Memoirs of the "Formosa Fraud"
## George Psalmanazar

Introduced and edited by Graham Earnshaw

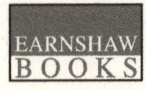

Memoirs of * * * *

The Memoirs of the "Formosa Fraud", George Psalmanazar

Edited by Graham Earnshaw

ISBN-13: 978-988-8422-28-9

This book has been reset in 10pt Book Antiqua. Spellings and punctuations are left as in the original edition.

HISTORY / Asia / Formosa

EB083

Published by Earnshaw Books Ltd. (Hong Kong)

# CONTENTS

have done if he had stayed in southern France and not written the Description.

In keeping with the age, the spelling and punctuation in this book are somewhat unruly. English spelling had been significantly standardized since the days of William Shakespeare, who died just sixty-three years before Psalmanazar was born, but the dictionary regimentation of Johnson and others had yet to be implemented. All spelling has been retained as in the original, but some punctuation has been altered, changing some semi-colons to commas and colons to periods.

Graham Earnshaw
China
2018

Mr George Psalmanazar.

# MEMOIRS of * * * *.

Commonly known by the Name of

## GEORGE PSALMANAZAR;

A

Reputed Native of FORMOSA.

Written by himself

In order to be published after his Death.

CONTAINING

An Account of his Education, Travels, Adventures, Connections, Literary Productions, and pretended Conversion from Heathenism to Christianity; which last proved the Occasion of his being brought over into this Kingdom, and passing for a Proselyte, and a Member of the Church of England.

---

LONDON:

PRINTED FOR THE EXECUTRIX.

Sold by R. DAVIS, in Picadilly; J. NEWBERY, in St. Paul's Church-Yard; L. DAVIS, and C. REYMERS in Holborn.

MDCCLXIV.

# ADVERTISEMENT

THE FOLLOWING SHEETS are printed for the benefit of Mr.
Psalmanazar's executrix; who thought it right to prefix his LAST
WILL AND TESTAMENT, as the best introduction to them. Mr.
Psalmanazar's first intimation of giving this public account
of himself, may be found under the article Formosa, in the
COMPLETE SYSTEM OF GEOGRAPHY, in which he assisted
as a writer. Where he was born, and who were his parents, do
not yet appear for certain; even in these posthumous memoirs
he has endeavoured to keep them inviolable secrets. From
circumstances however there is little reason to doubt, but that
he was a native of France: indeed he spoke the French language
so well, beyond what is usual when attained by grammar or
travel only, that we do not question to say, He was a Frenchman.
His pronunciation had a spice of the Gascoin accent, and in that
provincial dialect he was so masterly, that none but those born in
the country could equal, none though born there could excel him:
for notwithstanding it may be esteemed but a patois, or jargon,
yet foreigners find it impracticable to be spoken with propriety,
and with that fluency and vivacity peculiar to those people: and
from this we presume, that some part of Languedoc may lay
claim to his birth. The reverend Mr. Villette, who was intimately
acquainted with him for upwards of four and twenty years, (and
had many opportunities to observe him, and to know him well)
has communicated these conjectures, which the judicious reader,
perhaps, will see sufficiently confirmed from several passages in
the memoirs themselves.

# Psalmanazar's Will

THE LAST WILL AND TESTAMENT OF ME A POOR SINFUL AND WORTHLESS CREATURE COMMONLY KNOWN BY THE ASSUMED NAME OF GEORGE PSALMANAZAR

Thy ever blessed and unerring Will, Oh most gracious, though offended God! be done by me and all the world, whether for life or death.

Into thy all-merciful hands I commit my soul, as unto a most gracious Father, who, though justly provoked by my past vain, and wicked life, but more especially so during the youthful sallies of a rash and unthinking part of it, has yet been graciously pleased, by thy undeserved grace and mercy, to preserve me from the reigning errors and heresies, and the more deplorable apostacy and infidelity of the present age, and enabled me to take a constant and stedfast hold on the only author of our salvation, thy ever adorable and divine Son Jesus Christ, our powerful and meritorious Redeemer, from whose alone, and all-powerful intercession and merits (and not from any the least inherent righteousness of my own, which I heartily abhor as filthy rags in thine all purer eyes) I hope and beg for pardon and reconciliation, and for a happy resurrection unto that blessed immortality to which we are redeemed by his most precious and inestimable blood. I likewise bless and adore thy infinite goodness for preserving me from innumerable dangers of body and soul, to which this wretched life, but more particularly by my own youthful rashness and inconsideration, might have exposed me, had not thy Divine Providence interposed in such a

wonderful manner, as justly challenges my deepest admiration
and acknowledgment: particularly I am bound to bless thee
for so timely nipping that ambition and vainglory, which had
hurried me through such scenes of impiety and hypocrisy, and
as the most effectual antidote against it, next to thy divine grace,
hast brought me not only to prefer, but to delight in a state of
obscurity and lowness of circumstances, as the surest harbour
of peace and safety; by which, though the little I have left in
my possession be dwindled to so little value as to be but a poor
acknowledgment for the services which I have received from my
friend hereafter named, to whom I can do no less than bequeath
it all, yet I hope the will may be accepted for the deed, and that
the Divine Providence will supply to her what is wanting in me.
And now, O Father of Mercies, I beseech thee for thy dear Son's
sake, so to direct me by thy grace through all the future concerns
of this life, that when, where, or in what manner soever it shall
please thee to call me out of it, I may be found ready and willing
to return my soul, worthless as it is of itself, to thee who gavest it;
and my death, as well as my latter end, may be such as may tend
all possible ways to thy glory, the edification of thy church, and
my own eternal comfort. And in hopes there is nothing in this
my last will that is not agreeable to thine, I leave it to be executed
after my death by my worthy and pious friend Sarah Rewalling,
of this parish of St. Luke, in Middlesex, in the manner hereafter
mentioned, viz.

I desire that my body, when or whereever I die, may be kept
so long above ground, as decency or conveniency will permit,
and afterwards conveyed to the common burying-ground, and
there interred in some obscure corner of it, without any further
ceremony or formality than is used to the bodies of the deceased
pensioners where I happen to die, and about the same time of
the day, and that the whole may be performed in the lowest and

cheapest manner. And it is my earnest request, that my body be not inclosed in any kind of coffin, but only decently laid in what is called a shell of the lowest value, and without lid or other covering which may hinder the natural earth from covering it all around.

The books relating to the Universal History, and belonging to the Proprietors, are to be returned to them according to the true list of them, which will be found in a blue paper in my account book. All the rest being my own property, together with

all my houshold goods, wearing apparel, and whatever money shall be found due to me after my decease, I give and bequeath to my friend Sarah Rewalling above named, together with such manuscripts as I had written at different times, and designed to be made public, if they shall be deemed worthy of it, they consisting of sundry essays on some difficult parts of the Old Testament, and chiefly written for the use of a young Clergyman in the country, and so unhappily acquainted with that kind of learning, that he was likely to become the but of his sceptical parishioners, but being, by this means, furnished with proper materials, was enabled to turn the tables upon them.

But the principal manuscript I thought myself in duty bound to leave behind, is a faithful narrative of my education, and the sallies of my wretched youthful years, and the various ways by which I was in some measure unavoidably led into the base and shameful imposture of passing upon the world for a native of Formosa, and a convert to Christianity, and backing it with a fictitious account of that island, and of my own travels, conversion, &c. all or most of it hatched in my own brain, without regard to truth and honesty. It is true, I have long since disclaimed even publicly all but the shame and guilt of that vile imposition, yet as long as I knew there were still two editions of that scandalous romance remaining in England, besides the several versions it had abroad, I thought it incumbent upon me to undeceive the world, by unravelling that whole mystery of iniquity in a posthumous work, which would be less liable to suspicion, as the author would be far out of the influence of any sinister motives that might induce him to deviate from the truth. All that I shall add concerning it is, that it was began above twenty-five years ago with that view, and no other, during a long recess in the country, accompanied with a threatening disease, and since then continued in my most serious hours, as any thing new presented itself; so that it hath little else to recommend itself but its plainness and sincerity, except here and there some useful observations and innuendoes on those branches of learning in which I had been concerned, and particularly with such excellent improvements as might be made in the method of learning of Hebrew, and in the producing a more perfect body of Universal History, and more answerable to its title than that which hath already passed a second edition. And these, I thought, might be more deserving a place in that narrative, as the usefulness of them would in a great measure make amends for the small charge of the whole. If it therefore shall be judged worth printing, I desire it may be sold to the highest bidder, in order to pay my arrears for my lodgings, and to defray my funeral; and I further request that it be printed in the plain and undisguised manner in which I have written it, and without alteration or embellishment. I hope the whole is written in the true, sincere spirit of a person awakened by a miracle of mercy, unto a deep sense of his folly, guilt, and danger, and is desirous, above all things, to give God the whole glory of so gracious a change, and to shew the various steps by which his Divine Providence brought it about. The whole of the account contains fourteen pages of Preface, and about ninety-three more of the said relation, written in my own hand with a proper title, and will be found in the deep drawer on the right hand of my white cabinet. However, if the obscurity I have lived in, during such a series of years, should make it needless to revive a thing in all likelihood so long since forgot, I cannot but wish, that so much of it was published in some weekly paper, as might inform the world, especially those who have still by them the above-mentioned fabulous account of the Island of Formosa, &c. that I have long since owned both in conversation and in print, that it was no other than a mere forgery of my own devising, a scandalous imposition on the public, and such, as I think myself bound to beg God and the world pardon for writing, and have been long since, as I am to this day, and shall be as long as I live, heartily sorry for, and ashamed of.

These I do hereby solemnly declare and testify to be my last Will and Testament; and in witness thereof have thereto set my name, on the 23d day of April, in the year of our Lord 1752, O. S. and in the 73d year of my age.

G. Psalmanazar.

The last Will and Testament of G. Psalmanazar, of Ironmonger-Row, in the Parish of St. Luke, Middlesex, whenever it shall please God to take him out of this world unto himself.

January 1, 1762, being the day of the Circumcision of our divine Lord, then, blessed be God, quite sound in my mind, though weak in my body, I do ratify and confirm the above particulars of my last Will made.

# PREFACE

As the design of my leaving the following Memoirs, is at once to undeceive the world with respect to that vile and romantic account I formerly gave of myself, and of the island of Formosa, and to make all the amends in my power for that shameful imposition on the public, by leaving behind me this faithful narrative of myself, and of the remarkable accidents of my wretched life that led me to it, as well as of those that deterred me from persisting in it; it will not be improper here to premise some of the chief motives that determined me to write the following sheets, to be printed after my death.

The religious education I had happily received during my tender years, had made so strong an impression upon my mind, that, though it did not prove sufficient to preserve me from being unwarily and gradually hurried, by my own strong passion, into that scandalous piece of forgery; yet it never failed of making me condemn myself, in my more ferious hours, for every step I took towards it; but more particularly for the the last and most vile scene of all, my pretended conversion from Heathenism to Christianity, and the abominable means I was forced to use in order for it to gain credit in the world, so that I labored ever after under frequent and bitter remorses and stings of conscience, at the reflection of the great load of guilt into which I had suffered my youthful and unthinking vanity to hurry me.

And so much more deep was my sense of it, as I found my unhappy condition become so very difficult, and in some measure desperate, feeling nothing could effectually extricate me from it but a public acknowledgment of one of vilest and most odious impostures that youth and rashness could be guilt of, which I could not possibly have made, without exposing myself to shame and danger, and my friends to the deepest mortification and displeasure, and turning their underserved care and concern for me into the justest abhorrence and detestation of me.

Under these pungent reflections, which were, however, but too often smothered by various carnal considerations, and the violent hurry of my passions, I was not without some hopes that the same divine goodness, which had not suffered me to harden into an utter insensibility of my guilt, might, in his own good time, enable me to surmount all the dreadful difficulties which my carnal mind laid in my way, and finish that good work which my remorse gave me cause to hope was begun by his undeserved grace in me. I was not, however, without some apprehensions from a sense of my extreme guilt, lest that, which I cherished under the notion of hope, should prove only a vain and ill-grounded presumption, at least I began to fear I had reason to think it so, whilst I continued inactive, and depended merely on a few faint wishes and prayers, instead of making some strong resolutions and efforts, which might assure me of the divine grace co-operating with them.

In this fluctuating and wretched uncertainty I continued some years, not knowing which way to begin or go about the arduous and dreaded task, when a grievous and lingering fit of illness did, in some measure, hurry me to it, and made me determine immediately to set pen to paper, and employ all the time my distemper would allow me, to undo as much as was in my power all the mischief I had done, by leaving behind me a faithful account of every thing I could recollect, and that had been instrumental to so fatal and long a train of miscarriages, in order to set the whole imposture in so true a light, that no part of the shame may fall on the guiltless, but on the guilty; and that is chiefly on myself.

I set about it accordingly, and if I did not begin so necessary and laudable a work, till driven as it were to it by pain and sickness, by the fear of death, and of the divine displeasure, I hope it will be so far from lessening the credit of the following narrative, that it will rather add weight to it, seeing no time or circumstances can be more apt to inspire a man with the deepest seriousness and sincerity, than those I was in, when I wrote the most considerable and mortifying part of it.

I shall therefore only add, that my distemper was a lingering every-other-day ague, which lasted me about six weeks, and that being then in a sweet place of retirement in the country, at a very good friend's house, and taken sufficient care of in all other respects, I had all the time and opportunity I could wish for, joined with the properest disposition of mind for such a task, so that through God's blessing I was enabled to bring down the shameful account of my former unfortunate life through the most shocking and impious scenes of it, to my arrival into England without any interruption, and I hope in God with that sincerity and seriousness as such a relation could require, and my bad state of health could inspire me with, still taking care before all things to implore the divine assistance of the great searcher of all hearts every time I sat down to write, that he would direct me to go through the arduous task with such a due regard to truth, whatever shame reflected on me, as might in all respects redound to his glory, and entitle me to his pardon and mercy; and to him I give all the praise, for having enabled me not only to go on so far with the wished for work during my retreat there, but to resume it since at proper times, till I had brought it to the desired conclusion.

For being, soon after my recovery, obliged to return to London, and engaged in a work, which necessarily took up too much of my time and thoughts, to permit me to go on with this, in the same regular manner I had done in the country (though still resolved by God's assistance to go through with it) I determined to set apart an hour at least every Wednesday and Friday to revise what I had wrote, and to continue the narrative as my memory served; not doubting but the solemnity of the fast, joined to the prayers and other meditations I had appropriated for these two days, in the method of devotion I was through God's blessing entered into, would prove effectual means to

obtain that spirit of sincerity and seriousness which I earnestly wished might go through the remainder, as I was conscious it had done in the former part, whilst I laboured under my illness.

I went on accordingly for some time with it, till the other business I had in hand, and some other avocations, as well as sometimes an indisposition of the mind, unhinged me from my method oftener than I wished; for at such times I found myself so unfit to pursue it, that I plainly saw it was better to discontinue it till I could recover my former frame. This occasioned sometimes an intermission of two or more weeks as to the writing part, though the matter was still so pressing on my mind, that it only gave me an opportunity, either of recollecting some things I had omitted, or of gathering fresh materials for the sequel.

But as my aim was only to give an account of what either chiefly hurried me on through such a long train of the most unaccountable follies and vanities, or of what brought me to a sense and abhorrence of them, I have omitted a great number of the former, as rather apt to disgust than entertain or inform a sober reader, and confined myself to the latter, as the more likely to prove instructive and useful to him. And I shall not be very solicitous what judgment those will pass on this narrative, who are strangers to religion and the various ways of the Divine Providence in reclaiming sinners, first by driving, and then drawing them to himself, provided I can acquit myself to my own conscience that I have taken all possible care to write it with that sincerity and faithfulness that I would wish it to be done at my last moments, and with no other view than that of making such a full and ample acknowledgment of my great folly and guilt, as my conscience told me I ought to do for having so long and so shamefully imposed upon the world, as well as of God's singular goodness which inspired me with the design, and hath enabled me to go through it in the manner I have done.

The reasons of my not chusing to have it published during my life, besides those already hinted, will be seen in the sequel, and I hope will be thought solid and satisfactory, especially as it hath given me an opportunity of continuing the latter (and as I hope in God) the much better part of my life, and of adding to it several useful particulars, which the reader will find there; such as my easy and expeditious method of studying, and attaining to a fuller knowledge of the Hebrew tongue; sundry curious and instructive observations relating to some of the works I have been engaged in, in the learned way, particularly in that long and laborious one of the Universal History, of the design, beginning, and pursuit, together with the difficulties, miscarriages, faults, and other matters relating to both editions of it; and I have been the better able to give such an account of the whole as may be of use to the public, especially to the purchasers, as I have been concerned in it from the beginning.

The reader will likewise find the latter part of this narrative interspersed with many other particular accidents which have happily contributed not only to keep me steady in my resolutions and change of life, but which have likewise insensibly led me into a more regular way of thinking and acting; and, as true repentance begins in the change of the heart, and ends at the reformation of the sinner's life, I may humbly hope that I have not been negligent in finding out and using the most effectual helps and means, nor failed of the divine blessing on them, which are promised to all sincere penitents. Though the fear I was in, lest too particular an account of them should be deemed, by the censorious, as ostentatious and pharisaical, hath obliged me to conceal a great number of them, which might perhaps have otherwise proved very encouraging to people in my condition; not doubting but to those who are sincere in their repentance and resolutions, the same Divine Providence will suppeditate all the necessary helps and directions as their case requires, even as it hath graciously done to me.

All I would add by way of encouragement to persons in my unhappy circumstances (and worse or more dangerous no man could hardly be in than I was) is not to let the greatness of their guilt, or the difficulties of the duties of repentance, deter, but rather invite him to the throne of mercy, through the merits of our Divine Redeemer; for how dark and gloomy soever the prospect of so extraordinary a change may appear at first, as every thing doth to those that are fled from the broad sun-shine into some dark place; yet those thick and discouraging mists will gradually disappear, and every object that at first raised our fears will grow more hopeful and comfortable, when we call to mind that there is mercy sufficient in God, merits enough in Christ, power more than sufficient in the Divine Spirit, room enough in heaven, scope enough in the evangelical promises, and the most endearing invitations in the Gospel, to bring the greatest sinners to God of infinite mercy and compassion; so that there can be thenceforth no condemnation to them that, with faith and repentance, apply to him for pardon and grace through the merits of his ever-blessed Son, and use all proper means and helps to render himself a fit object of it.

We must not however suppose that the blessed effects of such a repentance will be so soon felt by us as we could wish, or that the duties of self-denial, self-abhorrence, fasting, solitude, meditation, self-examination, &c. will become easy and delightful as soon as we are entered into a religious regimen: we must, on the contrary, expect them to appear difficult and gloomy at the beginning, in order to excite our faith and reliance on the Divine assistance, which draws us not with an irresistible force, but with the cords of men, and the bands of love (Hos. xi. 4.) We must likewise expect to meet with frequent foils and backslidings in order to make us more diligent and watchful, more sensible of our own weakness, and more intent on that help which comes from above. By this means, we shall likewise be happily preserved from that pride and presumption, which is but too apt to insinuate itself into the minds of new converts; for experience plainly shews, that those two dangerous vices will be apt to spring, not only out of our sins and passions, but likewise out of our very virtues and graces, if not duly kept down, by the sense or experience of our own infirmities and impotence.

It was an excellent caution of a pious clergyman: "Don't presume; you are not yet come to a state of Christian perfection: don't despair; you are in the way to it." So that whatever difficulties or discouragements we may meet with in our progress, how short soever we may come of our duty, or whatever frailties, or even vices we may still be prone to, which may either divert or retard our speed, we may still comfort ourselves with the hopes, that we are in a way of growing better, and that the use of those means hath not only preserved us in a great measure from growing a great deal worse, but enabled us to rise after every fall, if it hath not sometimes made even those falls rebound to a greater heighth of grace, by teaching us, from every such step, to tread more sure for the future; and what a comfortable prospect must this yield to a man that hath made any progress in this happy way, to see God's strength magnified in his own weakness, especially when he adds thereto this blissful consideration, that the same all-meritorious blood which was shed to expiate all his wilful, if truly repented, transgressions, will much more effectually atone for all his involuntary defects.

Thus much I thought incumbent on me to say on this head, because whatever our

freethinkers may boast of the sufficient power of reason to reclaim a man from a long vicious course, from the prevalency of evil habits and constitutional vices, whatever powerful influence they may ascribe to the notion of eternal rectitude, &c. to reduce a man that hath deflected so wide and far from it, without any of those supernatural helps above-mentioned; yet I am well assured, that the former, without the latter, would have proved (to me at least, if not to any man in my condition) rather a determent than an effectual means; for what hopes or likelihood could there be that a wretch, who had, by his impetuous passion, been hurried into the commission of such a series of impieties against his own reason and conscience, should ever be able to extricate himself from such a slavish state by his own base natural power?

What efficacious help could he expect from his own reasoning faculties, which, however cried up by others, he had found, by sad experience, so weak and impotent, that the most they could do for him, was to make him condemn himself, without being able to rectify or resist the violent impulses of his predominant vice? Had, indeed, his knowledge of mankind furnished him with any remarkable instance of the prevalency of reason above a favourite vice, it might have given him some encouragement; but when he sees, on the contrary, that these strenuous despisers of all supernatural helps, equally enslaved to some favourite passion, and only differing from him perhaps in degree; the most he could expect his reason to do for him, would be to keep his own under some restraint and decorum, till time and indulgence had quite exhausted them.

But what poor encouragement is this to one in my dangerous case? how inconsiderable the change or remorse? what poor satisfaction to the world for so vile an imposition, and what likelihood that it would procure a pardon from an offended God, or calm the stings of a wounded conscience? And how much happier was it for me that I was directed to look up for and depend on a superior assistance, and instead of trusting to such a broken reed of my reason and strength, to apply myself to that Supreme Being, whose grace alone could work such an extraordinary change in the heart, give an effectual blessing on my weak efforts, and keep me steady in those resolutions which he had inspired me with, as well as in the use of those means he hath provided and prescribed to us!

I gladly repeat it, that nothing less than the hopes of his promised grace could have induced me to endeavour after it, and nothing but a full reliance on the merits of a Divine Intercessor could have invited me to cry to him for pardon and acceptance; and, on the other hand, nothing but the obtaining it could have supported me under my doubts and fears, my difficulties and discouragements, nor enabled me to persevere in, and nothing less than the continuance and increase of it could have brought a work of such extraordinary and undeserved mercy to perfection.

I cannot therefore but think it the greatest injury that can be done, to persons who have unhappily swerved from the paths of virtue and religion, to make them depend solely on the strength of their rational faculties for an effectual change, and to inspire them with a disregard for the more powerful means and motives which the Gospel offers to them, and which, upon experience, will be found the only ones that can bring it about. And may what I have here said inspire every awakened sinner, (who hath tried in vain the success of the former) with the more comfortable hope and stedfast confidence, in the never-failing efficacy of the latter.

Having said thus much on the subject of the divine grace offered to us in the Gospel, it will doubtless be expected that I should give some farther account of my private belief so far as relates to the controversy between the church of Rome, in which I was educated, and that of England, in the communion of which I have lived, ever since my coming into England. And here I must confess, to my very great shame, that though I did for several years profess myself a zealous member of the latter, yet the prejudices of my education, and the general course of my studies, did still strongly incline me in favour of the former; insomuch that neither the many books of controversy I had read on that subject, nor my frequent disputes with priests and others of that communion (in which, however, I had still vanity enough to give the preference to my arguments against it) could fix my wavering mind, much less could I be induced to think it so corrupt and dangerous, antichristian and idolatrous as it was with so much warmth maintained to be by most protestant writers and preachers; insomuch that this uncharitable zeal of theirs made me still more doubtful whether the reasons they urged were sufficient to justify their separation from it.

I was indeed sincerely persuaded, from all that I had read or heard, that the church of England was by far the best and safest of all the protestant churches; but that it was really more so than that of Rome, I was far enough from being satisfied in my mind; so that there was almost as little sincerity in my pretended zeal for and constant communion with it, than in my pretended conversion to it: the truth of it is, that I was too young and heedless, vain and conceited, to lie open to conviction, and that I read and heard the arguments on both sides, rather to fill my head than to rectify my heart, or fix my belief; so that I must confess that I acted at that time a very shameful and insincere part, in the preference I so strenuously gave to the one above the other, which, though ever so justly deserved, did not appear then in that light to me.

In this careless, though impious and abominable, suspence I continued some years (which, upon the whole, was but of a piece with the other and more flagrant part of my imposture) till I came to read a treatise, intituled, THE CASE STATED BETWEEN A NOBLEMAN OF THE CHURCH OF ROME, AND A GENTLEMAN OF THE CHURCH OF ENGLAND, in which I thought I found the controversy fully and clearly decided in favour of the latter. And I gave the heed to the arguments on both sides, not only as they appeared to me to be stated with the greatest clearness and impartiality, but as I had been long acquainted with Mr. Charles Lesley, the reputed author of that book, who was universally allowed to be one of the learnedest men in that controversy, and had moreover given the strongest proofs of his probity and sincerity, as well as of his capacity and unbiassed judgment; of all which I was so fully apprised, that no book that I had read did ever contribute so much, if not to fix my wavering mind, yet at least to make me think more seriously on the subject, and to give myself up to a fresh and more close application to that controversy, and the reading of all the best authors who had, or should afterwards write on either side; for I doubted not but we should soon hear of one or more answers from some of the best pens from that side, against it. However, though I never could learn of any that was made to it, it did not divert me from my purpose. And indeed I found myself so strongly prepossessed in favour of the author, that I had reason to fear lest the impression which his book had made upon my mind, should be owing to that, rather than to the validity of his arguments, until I had read over afresh all that had been urged in favour of the opposite side. But here again, though I went over them with the greatest attention and sincerity, I found the dispute so strangely managed, and clogged with such elaborate learning and sophistry, such controverted quotations from the Scriptures and ancient fathers, such unchristian charges of forgery, and perverting the sense of those authors, and other uncharitable language, as rather bewildered than convinced my mind; so that the only fruit I reaped from all my reading (besides a strong prejudice against those of the Romish side, whom I observed to deal most in that unfair way of disputing) was, that there could be no safety in trusting to my own judgment in a matter of such vast concern; and that it was next to impossible for men, frail as we are, and warped by our own passions and prejudices, to wade through such stormy seas of controversy, without an extraordinary assistance from the fountain of all light and truth. I have accordingly made it my constant care ever since, that is, for above these twenty-five years, to apply myself fervently, and to depend wholly upon that divine guide for a deliverance from all errors of faith and practice, and for such an increase of his light and grace as may confirm me in the belief of all his saving truths, obedience to all his commands, sincere communion with his holy catholic church, and a tender and charitable concern for all those who have swerved from it. To these petitions (which I constantly offered up to God, not only morning and night for a long series of years, but in a more copious and fuller form, suitable to my own exigence, on more solemn, that is, on fast and festival days) I hope is owing, that inward satisfaction which I have since been blessed with, in my more steady and sincere communion with the church of England, and in the preference I now give it to all other churches; and, as I hope in God, without the least breach of charity to any of the rest. And indeed by all that I have read, or been able to judge, I have been more and more convinced that theirs and ours are all in an imperfect state, though some more than others, and that they are like to continue so till the rising again of the sun of righteousness upon us, whose brightness will then enlighten at once both hemispheres, and who will then not only reform whatever is amiss in his mystical body, but bring the Jews, Turks, and Heathen into it; till then we can only in charity bewail whatever errors we see in them, either in faith or practice, and pray to God to reform them in his own good time, and to be merciful to those whose hearts are sincere towards him, whatever involuntary mistakes they may labour under.

Infallibility in the church were a blessing as much to be wished for in this uncertain state, as it is falsely challenged by the church of Rome; but since reason and experience shew it to be denied to us, and many sincere members of that church do privately bewail the errors that are crept into it, though loath to own them a sufficient cause for our separation from it, it highly becomes us all to make the best use of that guide which God hath given us, viz. his divine revealed Will and Word, without breaking the bond of Charity with those who interpret it in a different way from us: for though, in that respect, we may justly enough acknowledge in the words of our church's confession, that "we have" all, more or less, "erred and strayed like lost sheep," and that perhaps chiefly through our "following too much the devices and desires of our hearts;" yet as God is the only judge how far every man is faulty in that respect, should we not be very careful to pass such a favourable judgment on them, as may entitle us to the same indulgence from the judge of all hearts? Should it not at least (seeing we are all alike fallible, and stand in need of the same charitable allowance) make us exceeding fearful how we do, by our anathemas and other unchristian denunciations against those that differ from us, expose ourselves to the same severe sentence, and meet with the same measure at the last day, as we have so freely dealt unto them? This uncharitable condemning spirit, which hath so long reigned among Christians of all denominations, I have long since looked upon as the most dangerous error a man can fall into, as it is indeed the most open violation of the grand characteristic of the Gospel.

I have been ready to shudder when I have heard some of our preachers inveigh, in that uncharitable way, against their Fellow-christians, or even against our modern Freethinkers and Deists. Some of them I have heard and read, who could not speak or write of them without ridicule and derision, instead of that pity and concern which is due to persons in that dangerous state; and, for that reason, have always thought them the most unfit to teach others, who had all the true spirit of Christianity to seek, and can allow themselves to exult and droll over the errors and frailties of their fellow-creatures, which even common humanity forbids us to think of or mention without the utmost seriousness and compassion.

This uncharitable and untimely zeal, even in controversies of the highest nature, doth still more mischief in another way, by magnifying and aggravating the differences between the contending sides, which serves only to render them the more irreconcileable; whereas a true christian spirit will, from a sense of its own infirmity, rather chuse to excuse and palliate them, and will be extremely careful to soften and smooth every thing that is offered in the opposition, in order to render it less irksome and ineffectual.

Had our divine Lawgiver designed that we should have all agreed, in the main points of religion, or had he seen any thing so sinful and dangerous in our disagreement about it, his infinite wisdom and goodness would, doubtless, either have given us greater helps and brighter faculties, or would have taken care to have his revelation made so plain and obvious, that none but the wilful and perverse could have erred from it. In either of which cases, where would there have been any room for that charitable and forbearing spirit which is the peculiar characteristic of Christ's true disciples, and is so acceptable to him? not towards those that agreed with us from the same motives we agreed with them; nor yet much less towards those that differ from us, when it would have plainly appeared, that not their infirmity or ignorance, but their pride and perveseness made them do so. May we not therefore safely conclude, that God suffers us to continue in this imperfect and uncertain state, and unavoidable diversity of opinions, in order to give us an opportunity of exercising a virtue, which is of all others the most exalted and most acceptable to him, as being the nearest to its divine original.

God, who is emphatically stiled love, and hath been beyond all possible conception diffusive of it to us, hath, at the same time, assured us, that the best returns we can make to him for it, or he expects from us, is to make our own as extensive as we can to all that bear his divine image: herein therefore is this most excellent virtue, this charitable spirit displayed in a manner most nearly resembling his own, when (instead of treating those that differ from us with contempt, sourness, or impatience, which is base and selfish, or with ill language, opprobrious names, unjust reflections, curses, and anathemas, which is truly diabolical) we think and look upon them with the same candor, benevolence, and compassionate concern, as we should wish to be shewn to us were their case our own; when we make the most charitable allowances for their infirmities and mistakes, and are ready to ascribe their errors to the weakness of their understanding,

wrong education, or any thing rather than to the perverseness
of their will; when, by our behaviour, our prayers, and good
wishes, we strive to convince them that all our endeavours to
reclaim them from their errors, do really spring from our tender
sense of their danger, and from such a sincere and disinterested
concern for their spiritual welfare, as no opposition or obstinacy
on their part shall be able to lessen in the least, because that being
a duty enjoined by God, we cannot in any case dispense with
it, without danger of incurring his displeasure; and lastly, when
we can, in spight of all their obstinacy or untowardness, make
them sensible, by our words and deportment, that we wish their
happiness as heartily as ever; and that, after having tried our best
efforts in vain, we heartily recommend them still to that merciful
God, whose equity and goodness will acquit and approve every
man who conscientiously seeks for, and endeavours after the
best light, and is ready to obey it as far as he is able to observe it.

Could we once make this the aim and result of all our religious
differences and disputes, they would, instead of a bane, prove a
strong cement and support to Christianity; we might then differ
one from another without breach of charity, as friends love one
another, though of different tempers, complexions, &c. Our
unbelievers would be so far from taking an advantage from them
to cry it down, that they must be forced to admire and esteem it
for the blessed effects it produced in mens hearts and lives, how
wide soever their judgments differed in other cases; whereas,
whilst we make them the sad occasion of faction and strife, of
selfishness and malignity, or of unreasonable impositions on
the faith and practice, of slander, hatred, persecution, &c. it can
hardly be expected that our sceptics and infidels will be candid
or ingenuous enough to perceive, or at least to own, that all this
unchristian behaviour is diametrically opposite to the Gospel.

It is indeed much to be wished, that some of the ancient

fathers had not mingled so much of this antichristian spirit with their otherwise pious and learned writings, and had not done, as the great St. Jerome owns himself, in his epistle to Pammachius; to have done against Jovinian, that he had less regarded what was exactly to have been urged against him, than what might be laid as a charge against him. How much of our now reigning scepticism and infidelity may have been owing to such an unchristian spirit, propagated and improved as it hath been in subsequent ages, and how much such uncharitable writers and preachers of controversy will have to answer for it at the last day, I will not presume to determine; but thus much I may venture to infer from it, that those Boanerges did chuse the most unlikely means of recommending Christianity to the unbelieving part of the world, (if such was their real design) when they strove to propagate it in a way so diametrically opposite to the meek and benevolent spirit of its divine author.

This single consideration, joined to the sense had of the weakness of our understanding and incapacity of judging in matters of so high a nature, hath long ago made me very careful of condemning or censuring any church or sect for holding any tenets which my conscience could not readily join in. We may indeed expose ourselves to a severer judgment, by passing too rash or uncharitable a one on others, but can never run the same risk by the most candid and favourable allowance we can make for them. And, after all, what have we to do to judge those that differ from us, since both they and we must stand accountable to him only who is the unerring judge of all hearts?

I cannot forbear adding, that the almost unsurmountable difficulties I have found to come to the bottom of the greater part of our disputed points, and the little certainty or satisfaction I have reaped from reading of most controversies, clogged and disguised as they are with sophistry and endless subtilities, and managed with so little appearance of impartiality and charity, have made me such a Pyrrhonian in polemic divinity, that I have not dared to allow myself the liberty of censuring those who held what I thought an error in faith or practice, or even to pronounce it to be such, though I have been wanting in neither zeal nor courage to oppose any such on all proper occasions, and to give the best reason I could for my dissenting from them; and I much question whether, in the imperfect and uncertain state we are in, reason or religion will permit us, much less require of us, to proceed farther; and whether a more positive or categorical declaration doth not argue something worse than prepossession and narrowness of mind, and will not be liable to be condemned as an unchristian warp of the will.

The transubstantiation of the church of Rome, is a doctrine that appears the most shocking to sense and reason. That of absolute predestination among the greater part of the reformed churches, appears not only the most opposite to the divine attributes of love, goodness, justice, &c. but to strike at the root of the Christian religion, which is founded on the love of God; for how is it possible for a man to look upon so arbitrary a being as that doctrine represents him, but with the utmost awe and dread, even though he was ever so fully persuaded that himself was one of the predestinate? and how much more so the more he is removed from such a persuasion? Nevertheless, as I have all possible reason to believe that there are myriads of men of learning and probity who behold those two doctrines in a quite different light, and not only hold them as necessary articles of their faith, but are ready to condemn all that do not, why should I be so partial to my own judgment, as to think it more infallible than theirs, or venture to pass the same uncharitable sentence on them for believing which I blame them in my conscience for pronouncing against me for not believing them?

With what justice can I charge the former with idolatry for worshipping what they sincerely believe to be the real body of our divine and adorable Redeemer? Or how can I tax the latter with impiety for professing a doctrine, which I ought in charity to think they would abhor, did it appear to them as derogatory of God's goodness and justice, as it doth to me, especially as the belief of both is founded on their implicit belief, (and consequently, and at the worst, on a mistaken interpretation) of the Holy Scripture?

Is it not therefore more safe and more christian for me to content myself with giving my reasons in the strongest manner I am able, for my dissent from them, than to charge them, even in thought, with wilfully perverting the word of God, and with all the guilt and infamy of imposing damnable errors, under pain of damnation? It may be indeed truly said, that this kind of retaliation is what not only reigns too much in most christian churches, even to this day, but hath proved the frequent occasion of the most horrid persecutions and antichristian cruelties: But is it not therefore the more to be avoided and abhorred by all true Christians for the mischief it hath done, and is still able to do, to the Gospel, and for the scandal it reflects on the best religion in the world?

Ought it not to be a matter of the deepest grief and concern to a good Christian, to see the most gracious designs of heaven towards mankind thus miserably obstructed and frustrated, and so great a part of mankind deprived of the inestimable benefits of it, by an untimely zeal, the most opposite to the spirit of our meek and divine Redeemer, and the most condemned, both by his precepts and example? Doth not right reason itself, as well as our natural self-love, tell every man how careful he ought to be not to be mistaken in a matter of such infinite concern? And suppose we have ever so much reason to think those that differ

33

from us are really so, must we therefore take upon us to censure and condemn, to anathematize and persecute them, whom reason and charity should rather incline us to pity and pray for, whether their error be wilful or involuntary, which can only be known to God?

I have chosen to instance in the doctrines of transubstantiation and predestination, as they appear the most shocking and antiscriptural to every one, except those who believe them; nevertheless, from a sense of my fallibility, as well as of the weakness of human reason, I should be very fearful of pronouncing them absolutely false (much less to call them anti-christian, damnable, &c.) their appearing so to me is a sufficient reason for my declaring my dissent from them, but doth not authorize me to pronounce those that believe them to be guilty before God for so doing.

Were I to indulge myself in the liberty of censuring or condemning any christian church, for any thing either in their faith or practice, it would be that uncharitable authority they assume of condemning, as hereticks, &c. all those who cannot believe as they do.

And yet I own it highly necessary that there should be, in every particular church (since it is not given to us in this imperfect state to be thus happily united in our belief) a stated rule of faith, a summary of what is to be principally believed and practised by all its members; but then care should be taken not to multiply those articles beyond what is absolutely necessary, nor yet to impose them with any such damnatory clauses against recusants as are commonly used by most churches, to the great detriment and discredit of Christianity, and the intimidating and bewildering the sincere and well-meaning Christians, who are incapable of judging of the merit of those controversies, and being commonly by far the most numerous, are entitled to

34

a more charitable and tender regard than to be obliged blindly to believe and act as their church prescribes, or be liable to be rescinded from it.

Even in those articles wherein our church is obliged to declare its dissent from any of the tenets of others, methinks they might and should in charity content themselves with giving their reasons, in the plainest and concisest manner, for their dissent, and with such impartial candor and tenderness as should rather inspire its members with pity and concern for, than prejudice and hatred against, those that differ from them: and, above all things, they should all be exceedingly fearful of charging their antagonists, and their tenets, with a greater degree of guilt and danger than is consistent with truth, and with that spirit which condemns and abhors all misrepresentation and opprobrious language as the most destructive, next to ill offices or persecution, of all errors that a Christian can fall into.

It is plainly the want of this meek christian spirit, that makes men to intermix so much deadly acrimony in all their disputes and differences, as serves only to destroy the small sparks of charity that are left among us. But where the love of Christ unites our hearts in the bonds of peace and mutual benevolence, no difference in religion, however greatly misrepresented or aggravated by untimely zeal, will ever be able to dissolve the tye, or create the least disagreement or indifference in their affections.

There are many things in the Greek, and Roman church, in that of Geneva, and Augsburgh, &c. which my conscience will not permit me to join with; but which I, at the same time, firmly hope and believe will not be laid to their charge by the merciful searcher of all hearts, who rather pities than punishes the involuntary errors of his frail creatures: and were there none better to be found in the christan world than those, I should think myself obliged to join communion with that which appeared to me the freest from them, rather than to stand by myself, and be deprived of the benefit of church-fellowship, provided nothing was imposed upon me by it that my conscience thought sinful. I look upon them all (excepting such as deny the fundamental articles of Christianity, especially the merits and mediation of our divine Redeemer) as so many branches of Christ's church; and tho' some are more corrupted than others, yet all united into one body, of which he himself is the supreme head and governor, and is acknowledged by them as such.

However, I own that the church of England hath, in all respects, appeared to me, ever since I have made myself more seriously acquainted with its faith and practice, the best reformed and freest from every thing that could restrain me from her communion, especially as I am a layman: for with respect to her clergy, I think some of the injunctions she lays them under to be such as I could by no means submit to, and which the more conscientious among them would, I believe, be glad to be freed from, if it could be done consistently with the honour, and safety of its establishment. I am far from intending by this to cast any blemish on the reverend order, or on the first reformers; but as it hath given so much occasion for cavil and disrespectful reflections against both, I could heartily wish to see it effectually removed. In other respects I have long since had a vast esteem and regard for her liturgy, sacraments, ordination, and other ordinances, that it hath been, and is still, a matter of regret to me, whenever business or any other impediment hath deprived me of the benefit of them.

Her episcopacy, though so much disregarded by other protestant churches, and cried down, as invalid, by that of Rome, hath long ago been looked upon by me, not only as a singular blessing, but as a necessary constituent of a church, the divine institution of which hath been, in my opinion, as fully proved against the former, as the validity of its ordination hath against the latter; and all I have to wish for her sake, is, that she was as happy in the choice, appointment, and promotion of her prelates; and that the Congès Delire were something more than a phrase without meaning: however, that needs not to debar us, in this imperfect state, from enjoying the benefits of their sacred function to very good purposes; nor discourage us from wishing and praying for a reformation of those abuses which worldly politicians have introduced into it.

Most people indeed, who look upon the evil to lie in human nature itself, have little hopes to see any amendment to it, till we have a new heaven and a new earth, especially as those in whose power the remedy is, are most interested to suppress it: But a good Christian will look higher up than those at the helm for so desirable a change, since, as I believe, we have much more reason to hope for it from the interposition of heaven, than any of the neighbouring churches which labour under the same difficulties. As for those countries abroad, which have secularized their bishopricks, &c. they will hardly charge our church with abusing hers worse than they have done theirs; so that, upon the whole, it appears in all respects to stand upon a better and more hopeful foot than any other I know, with all its imperfections and defects.

I cannot dismiss this point without taking some notice of a charge which some of our present Methodists have laid to it, viz. its having departed from some of its ancient doctrines, particularly those of predestination and free-grace, or imputed righteousness. With respect to the former, it doth not appear that the compilers of the seventeenth article ever designed to impose the belief of it as necessary to salvation, but only to define the term of predestination, as strenuously maintained by the reformed churches of Geneva, Switzerland, Holland, &c. leaving it to the option of every one either to assent or dissent from it: much less

37

do they seem to have insisted upon the belief of it in that full and extensive sense (and including absolute reprobation) in which the Supralapsarians explain it, which doctrine is now justly rejected by most divines and members of this church. Mr. Whitefield's charge of innovation is therefore unjust; and it is well known, that he did not think otherwise of it, till he was persuaded into that opinion upon his going to preach in America: however, could it be supposed that the first reformers really designed it in that supralapsarian sense, I should have commended any synod who should have since then ordered it to have been erased, seeing the truth of a christian doctrine is not founded on the opinion or authority of any men, but on the evidence of Holy Writ.

With respect to the other charge, viz. inherent and imputed righteousness, it must be owned, that our sermons and books of devotion seem rather to run so much in commendation of good works, as to lead people to lay a greater stress on the former than on the latter, and to confide more on their good deeds than on the merits of Christ, which is certainly a dangerous mistake, since our hope of acceptance and salvation must be chiefly founded upon the latter, without which our best duties could never be acceptable from such frail and sinful creatures to a God of infinite holiness.

It were therefore to be wished, that our preachers and divines would take some more care to caution their hearers and readers, whenever they insist on the necessity of good works, against their putting their chief dependence on them, and to remind them that the alone merits and intercession of our divine Redeemer can give them their saving efficacy. But though this last point is not so frequently inculcated and insisted upon as could be wished, yet that it is always understood and implied, is certain, because it always was, and is still acknowledged to be a fundamental article of the church of England; so that it is unjust to charge it with having departed from it; and yet this is the common cry of these modern enthusiasts, who are every where denouncing damnation against all those who insist on or put any dependence on inherent righteousness: but how unjustly and falsely, let the apostle St. Paul inform them, who expresly tells us (1 Corinth. iii. 11-15.) that such men shall be saved, though with great difficulty; or, as he expresses it, so as by fire, though not one of their works should stand the fiery trial; for how precarious soever the superstructure be, whilst Christ is the foundation, he cannot but be safe that builds his hopes upon it, whatever straw, stubble, or other trash he may intermix with it.

However, I do not doubt but this false alarm of the Methodists hath proved of some use to many Christians, as I own it hath to me, and hath awakened them into a better and humbler opinion of their inherent righteousness, than they perhaps had before. As to my own particular, tho' I always depended solely on the merits of a crucified Redeemer for pardon and acceptance, and looked upon all our best services to be destitute of the least worth, but what they receive from him; yet I have been warned, by this late outcry, to put less stress and confidence in them, and to look upon them rather as the evidence of our sincerity and salvation, than as the means or foundation of it, rather as our qualification for heaven (on which account we may safely wish, endeavour, and pray that we may more and more abound in them) than as things capable to give us any title to it, which nothing can do but the imputed righteousness of Christ.

Thus much I thought incumbent on me to declare concerning my notions of religion in general, of the church of England in particular, and my reason for preferring her communion to all other. I hope they are all agreeable to the word of God, and that I have taken all possible care and pains to have them chiefly founded on that, by frequently reading and consulting the sacred volumes in their original, and using all proper helps, as commentators, paraphrasts, books of controversy, &c. in order to come at their true meaning. But above all, my chief dependence hath been upon the guidance and assistance of God's Holy Spirit, which, for a great number of years, I have never failed daily to implore, as I was truly sensible, how poor and insignificant all other helps would be without it, towards the bringing us through the vast mazes of controversy, which reign all over Christendom, to the wished-for haven and salvation, to which I earnestly pray to God to bring every sincere soul, that longs and strives for it. I firmly rely on the same divine goodness to whom I owe so many mercies, and so wonderful a change, that if there be yet any thing erroneous or amiss, either in my belief and practice, he will, in his own time, and by his all-sufficient light and grace, enable me to rectify it, that I may have nothing left to do but to acknowledge and adore his infinite and undeserved mercies to me, and particularly for having enabled me to see so much of my own weakness and insufficiency, unworthiness and misery, as to put my whole trust and confidence in his all-powerful grace and unbounded goodness, through the infinite merits of our blessed Redeemer.

Before I conclude this Preface, it will be likewise necessary for me to give some account of that vast quantity of laudanum I have been known to take for above these forty years, and my motives for so doing, in order to undeceive such persons as may have conceived too favourable an opinion of that dangerous drug, from any thing they may have heard me say, heard at secondhand, or may have observed of the small visible hurt I have received from it, during so long and constant a use of it.

And first of all, as to the true occasion of my taking it, whatever pretence I may heretofore have made for it, such as its easing the pain of the gout, (which distemper, though I heretofore pretended to be often troubled with, yet I never was, nor had the least symptom or tendency to in my constitution) or of its being a great help to study, a reviver of the spirits, and the like, which qualities it in some measure hath; yet my motive for taking it at first, and continuing it so long, was no other than my vanity and senseless affectation of singularity; and as that was then my predominant passion, so I indulged it in this and many other such extravagant ways, at any hazard, as the following sheets will more fully shew.

Secondly, as to the quantity, though it never came up to that vast excess as I did then pretend; yet I own that I frequently took such large doses, by way of ostentation, as must have proved detrimental, if not quite fatal, to any man that had had a less strong and happy constitution than I was blessed with; and I have been very often surprised to find that I received so little prejudice from it. And this it was that emboldened me to take such large and dangerous draughts of it, without the least necessity or motive for it, but to be taken notice and talked of; insomuch that I continued it during such a number of years, that I was become a perfect slave to, and could not be easy without it, tho' I had for some time been sensible of the ill consequences attending the constant use of it, especially as often as I indulged my vanity with a larger dose than usual.

Thirdly, As to my vain pretence of having found an effectual way of stripping the opium of all its pernicious qualities, though it was true in part, and I had fallen upon a preparation of it (which was a kind of safe and useful improvement on that which Dr. Jones gives us in his MYSTERY OF OPIUM) by the help of some acids, particularly the juice of Seville oranges, which, mixed with some alcalies, raised a kind of ferment in the infusion, by which some of the most viscous and narcotic parts were either scummed off, or made to subside; yet so far was it from being so inoffensive and beneficial, as I gave it out, that I had frequent occasion to observe some of its ill effects in those whom I unadvisedly persuaded to use it in some proper cases, as I thought, so that I was obliged to leave off prescribing it to others; though, as to myself, I was a long while before I found any inconvenience in taking it, even in that large quantity; and I have great reason still to think it less dangerous by far than either that of Dr. Sydenham's, or any infusion exhibited by the apothecaries and common dispensaries.

However, when I began to feel the inconvenient effects of it, which was not till a good number of years using it, I thought it high time to lessen the usual dose (which was then about ten or twelve tea spoonfuls morning and night, and very often more) as fast as I conveniently could, and in about six month's time had reduced myself to half an ounce per day, and somewhat weaker than the common Sydenham. I still continued decreasing; but such was my foolish vanity, that, to conceal my reduction, I added some other bitter tincture, especially that of hierapicra, or some other such corrective, among it, to appear as still taking my usual quantity.

On the other hand, I found that this reduction, gradual as it was, could not be continued without some affecting and discouraging inconveniences; such as a great lassitude and uneasiness of the mind, an indolence and incapacity for study, a dislike to every thing I read or wrote, to solitude and application; all which made me apprehensive, that if I did not slacken it, and go more warily on with it, I might bring myself into a greater evil than that which I endeavoured to shun, and fling myself at length into a kind of habitual torpor and inactivity, which might prove at least as detrimental to me: to prevent which, I was forced to take a new method, and to inlarge or lessen my dose, according to the state of health I was in, sometimes according as the weather was more or less enlivening, or according as the course of my studies required a greater or lesser degree of application. All this, however, was rather owing to my own natural indolence and want of resolution to go on in spight of all those inconveniences, than to any danger there really was in the case, as I happily found reason afterwards to think; for when the Divine Providence was pleased to bless me with a contrary turn of mind, and to make me detest and abhor all my former follies, and this among the rest, to such a degree, as to resolve, by his assistance, upon a thorough change, I then found both the task, and all the inconveniences attending it, to grow more and more easy; and as this resolution was founded upon a much better principle than my former ones were, so it was attended with such a blessing at my last stay at Oxford, anno − − from July to the latter end of September, by which time I had made a considerable progress in my reduction, that I had quite completed the conquest, and lived some weeks there without taking one drop, or even wishing for it, although neither then nor since was I without some employment which required a pretty close application.

In this pleasing state, as I justly thought it, I continued for some months, when the severity of the ensuing winter overturned all my measures, and forced me, though much against my will, to have recourse to it again: neither could I think of any safer or more effectual remedy against that chilness of my blood, and lowness of spirits, which I laboured under through the excessive coldness of the season. I resolved, however, to resume it in the smallest quantity that I could find would answer my end; that is, what was, as near as I could judge, equivalent to ten or twelve drops of Sydenham's, and with full intention to leave it off as soon as the warm weather returned, and had accordingly reduced myself to about half that quantity, though not without some difficulty, on account of a work I was still engaged in, and the necessity we were under to keep time with the printers and publishers. Finding it at length so necessary and pleasant, as well as safe and harmless, I resolved to continue it, and have done so to this present time; that is, for seven or eight years, without the least inconvenience from it. On the contrary, I have reason to think that even that small quantity, though scarce equivalent to twelve drops of Sydenham's, hath been of some service to me to prevent that decay of spirits which old age, (being now drawing near my seventieth) a sedentary life, and close study, might otherwise probably have brought upon me: and it is to this small dose, which I take every night in a pint of very small punch, as soon as I leave off writing, that I attribute, next to the blessing of God, that good share of health I have hitherto enjoyed, and my having been able, for so many years, to go through the fatigues and applications of study, from seven in the morning to seven at night, preserving still a good appetite and digestion, a clear head, and tolerable flow of spirits, and enjoying a sound sleep of six or seven hours, without indulging myself in any other liquors than tea all the day, and the abovementioned quantity of punch, or something equivalent to it at night; and as I have not opportunity for much exercise, I take care to live on the plainest diet at noon, and to observe the old adage at night,

*Ut fis nocte levis, fit tibi caena brevis.*
To sleep easy at night, let your supper be light.

# Memoirs,
## Of
## George Psalmanazar.

I CANNOT BETTER begin this melancholy account of my former
life, vile and abominable as it hath been, and blended with
such mixture of the most unaccountable pride, folly, and stupid
villainy, in opposition to reason, religion, and all checks of
conscience, till almost to the thirtieth year of my age, than by
humbly acknowledging the infinite mercy of God, not only
in preserving me so long from the many evils and disasters
which my own wicked rashness must else unavoidably have
precipitated me into, as the sequel will sufficiently show; but
much more so in that gradual and visible change which his grace
wrought in me, by enabling me frequently to retrospect with
shame and remorse on a life so basely spent, to send up the most
fervent wishes to heaven that I might at length break off from so
shameful and wicked a course of the vilest and most scandalous
imposture, that a wild and abandoned youth could be guilty of,
and that I might but be blessed with such a steady resolution
as at once publickly to disclaim all the lies and forgeries I had
formerly published in that monstrous romance, and at any rate
or risk to take the shame to my self, and make a free confession
of the whole imposture. But I had not only my pride to combat,
but the displeasure which such a declaration would give to all
my friends, who being very honest and religious, could not but

have taken it much at heart, and, perhaps, been exposed to the

censure of the world for their charitable opinion of me; to say nothing of the abhorrence they must have conceived-against so detestable a cheat. As these therefore were such powerful determents to a man wholly destitute of any laudable way of living, I could not expect that my earnest wishes would be speedily answered; and my only hope was, that the same gracious God, who had thus effectually awaked me to a sense of my guilt and danger, would also in his own time hear those prayers which himself had inspired me to make, especially, as upon a retrospection of my past follies, I was apt to comfort myself with the thoughts, that the violence of my favourite passion, pride, could never have hurried me so irresistibly through such scenes of folly and danger, if there had not been some sad flaw in my understanding, some unavoidable degree of madness in my temper, which might in some measure extenuate, if not wholly excuse, the atrocious guilt it had involved me in; and the hope that it might still be placed to that account, by a merciful Judge of all our thoughts and intents, of our frail and corrupt nature, joined to the stedfast confidence I had in the promises of the Gospel, and in the infinite merits of a divine Saviour, preserved me from despairing of mercy and pardon, of success and blessing on those happy beginnings, if closely and earnestly pursued.

But as such a hope, without a sincere desire of doing one's part, to the best of one's power, and according to the degree of assistance given from above, would rather deserve the name of rash and shameful presumption; so the next step I took, at least in view, was to set about making all possible reparation to God and his church, and to the world, and my own conscience, for the scandal which such a vile piece of hypocrisy must have given to all, especially to good men, and in spite of all reluctance from pride and self-love, which the greater it was, would the more naturally lead one to the throne of mercy for a proportionable supply of Divine grace, and patiently to wait for it in God's own proper time. I had not continued many months in this hopeful disposition, before I perceived all those difficulties and discouragements to vanish by degrees, but more especially at the approach of a severe disease, though lingering, and the apprehensions of death, which last, as it did not appear to be so near at hand, gave me room to hope I might have time sufficient granted me in mercy, to go through this faithful narrative, and undeceive the world; so that if the Divine Providence did think fit to drive me to the writing of it by his afflicting hand, I hope it will rather add weight to the credit of it, seeing no time is fitter than this to inspire a man with the deepest seriousness and sincerity. But as to me, I still more rely on the assistance of that spirit of truth, to whose special grace I am bound to ascribe the abhorring sense I had already conceived against my former guilt, as well as the earnest desire and resolution of transmitting to the world such an account of my past guilty life, as might wholly contradict and explode that false and impious one, which I had been induced to publish in the days of my abominable folly and vanity. Under that Divine Guide therefore I set myself immediately about it, and carried on daily, and with as much application as my disease (a very violent ague and fever) would permit, not doubting but the sincerity which I resolved, by God's assistance, should reign through the whole, would make some amends for the lowness of stile, and other imperfections, which, considering my weakly condition both of mind and body, were in some measure unavoidable. Thus far I thought necessary to apprise the reader concerning the (happy, I hope I have reason to call it) occasion of my writing the following account, which in the name, and under the direction of that same God of truth, I now hope to live to see finished, in order to be printed, if thought worthy of it, after my death; and I shall only add, that I am at this present time of writing (April 22, 1728) at a friend's house in the country, free from all study and business, or any other impediment, but what is caused by my distemper, and shall dedicate all the time I have to spare in the writing of it.

But here I hope I shall be excused from giving an account either of my real country or family, or any thing that might cast a reflection upon either, it being but too common, though unjust, to censure them for the crimes of private persons, for which reason I think myself obliged, out of respect to them, to conceal both. Out of Europe I was not born, nor educated, nor ever travelled; but continued in some of the southern parts of it till about the sixteenth year of my age, when necessity obliged me in some measure to remove into more northern ones, though never farther northward than the Rhine in Germany, or Yorkshire in England. And this I purposely mention, because I have been heretofore suspected to be a German, Swede or Dane by some; by others, an English or Scotchman, as their fancy lead them, though I never saw Germany till I was sixteen, nor England till about two or three years after. As for my parents and relations they were Roman Catholics, and most of them very zealous in their way, and strongly biassed against all Protestants. My father was of an ancient, but decayed family, and had been obliged to leave my mother before I was five years old, and to live near five hundred miles from her, whilst she was left to live and breed me up upon her small fortune, without receiving any assistance from him, his misfortunes having put it quite out of his power to contribute any thing; so that I was wholly left to her care. However, neither that, nor the narrowness of her circumstances, hindered her from giving me the best education she could, being then her only surviving child. She was a pious good woman in her way, and though I was no small favourite of hers, was yet kept with due strictness whilst I staid with her, which was however but a short time, and do not remember that I had then any the least vicious inclination, nor in all likelihood might have had, had I still continued under her wing; whereas through the mismanagement of those first persons to whose tuition I was next committed, such a wrong foundation was laid, and so strong a biass given me to vanity and self-conceit, as proved the unhappy source of all my sad miscarriages since.

One general remark here I cannot avoid making concerning the schools of the Roman Catholics, viz. that all their students must learn to read, and even pray, in Latin, before they are capable of understanding one word of it; for this doth but inure them to read and pray without any attention, even when they are afterwards capable of understanding what they read and pray for. This ill-timed method had been complained of by many a one who have since felt the sad effects of it, as well as the almost insurmountable difficulty of mastering a defect so early contracted and so deeply rooted, as it were, in our nature, and none hath had more reason to bewail it than I.

But what did me in particular the most hurt, in my education abroad, was the great admiration which my more than common readiness at learning whatever came in my way had gained me, and the imprudent fondness and partiality which my masters shewed to me on that account. I was hardly turned of six years when I was sent to a free-school taught by two Franciscan monks, the eldest of whom perceiving my uncommon genius for languages, for till then I had only learned to read all sorts of print and writings, and was besides very careless about writing a tolerable hand, took it into his head to put me to the Latin form, though my mother and all my friends thought me much too young for it, especially as I was to be ranked and classed among other boys of twice my years, and who had already been at it a year or two, and some more; however he depended so much on his judgment, about my genius and application, that he doubted not, he said, but to see me out-top all the rest in less than a year or two.

He was not mistaken, and though it put me to great difficulties and hard study to reach them, I began to feel such emotions of vanity at the quick progress I made, and the commendations he gave me upon it, that I rested not satisfied till I had gained the first rank in the form, as well as in his affection, for as he spared neither caresses nor encouragement to me, I soon became sensible both by his behaviour, as well as by the deference which the other boys paid to me, how much I was got in his favour.

Our school was often visited by priests, monks, gentlemen, and other persons that passed through our city, and though we had in it several boys whose parents were in a much higher station, yet I was always singled out as the flower of the flock, and as the most ready to answer such questions as were suitable to our form. Our monk had likewise, by way of animating us, caused some curious nicknacks to be made by the nuns of a neighbouring monastery, which they were to wear hanging to their button-holes, by a fine ribon, who held the first seats. These were of several sizes, and one of them much larger than the rest was for the foremost in rank. We were to be entitled to these according to our merit, and this last fell to my lot from the first exercise, and so proud was I become of this bauble, that I never lost it for one single day; for I had such a ready and retentive memory, and quick apprehension, as by the help of a moderate application, made it impossible for my school-fellows to wrest it from me. This mark of distinction did moreover entitle me to be head monitor and marshal of that whole school. All which filled me with such vanity and ambition to excel, that I could not brook any superiority or preference, and our monk was but too fond of indulging, and even encouraging me in it, though to my no small detriment, as he might easily perceive that it had given me such a strong bias to pride, as a prudent man would have rather chosen to nip in the bud, especially as he easily perceived that it created no small envy in my school-fellows, and a kind of dissatisfaction in some of their parents and relations.

He tried once indeed to thwart his partiality to me, by giving our form a new kind of exercise, the price of which to the best performer was to be a fine piece of nun's work, which he adjudged to another, whom all the school knew to be a dunce, but in point of quality the head of us all. Had he given it to some others of our form, who were greater proficients in learning, I might have thought they had succeeded better in their performance than I at that time; and though it would have been a great mortification to me, it might have only made me double my diligence; but here the preference was so flagrant and visible, that I could not forbear expressing a desire to know wherein he had outdone me, and a suspicion that he had been assisted underhand by some monk or somebody else. When the good father found that I took the matter so to heart, and, in some measure, threaten to bid adieu, if not to the Latin, at least to his school; (and I believe I should really have done it, so highly I resented what I called the injustice done me) he thought fit to pacify me by assuring me, that my competitor had, upon this occasion, so far excelled himself, that he could not forbear assigning him the prize by way of encouragement, though my performance was far enough from being inferior to his; and so, to put an end to the contention, immediately sent for another piece of the same curious work, and gave it to me, not without some great encomium on my uncommon diligence and progress, and other tokens of his singular regard, which sent me home so satisfied and full of myself, that, alas for me! every thing seemed to contribute to swell my growing pride, and make me forget myself.

Many other such instances of his partial fondness I could name, which all tended to make me still more assuming and arrogant; one however I cannot pass by, which shall serve as a specimen: as I never was guilty of a fault at school, so let me do what I would out of it, I was never punished for it, as the other boys were, but had, perhaps, a soft reprimand or some easy task assigned me by way of penance, for I cannot call to mind that I ever had a blow or cross word from him. One day in particular, some strangers, who visited us after dinner, obtained us a discharge for the rest of the day. We were no sooner got out but I told my school-fellows, that we ought to go and procure the same release to the girls of another school. Accordingly we went and broke into the house, and drove the mistress and scholars out, and then locked the doors, that they might not be obliged to come in again, and sent her the key at night. On the next day a severe complaint was brought against us for the assault, and I charged as the ringleader of the rest, upon which a suitable punishment was promised, and soon after put in execution, in which I not only expected to have a share, but to be the first called down to it, and yet by what partial motive I know not, I had no other punishment than a seeming severe reprimand, and some easy task, whilst all the rest were forced to submit to the discipline of the school. This partiality they loudly complained of, not only to him, but to their friends; but their resentment upon it only gave me new matter for triumph, as it did to them new cause for envy, which yet they dared not vent in any other way than words.

Thus I went on learning of Latin apace, I could translate out of it, write and speak it with great readiness, as far as I had been taught, which was thought surprising, considering I had hardly attained my ninth year, and been but two years under his care. The misfortune was, that he made us only conversant with common school-books, and but with few of any of the old classics either in prose or verse, so that I was quite unacquainted with their stile till I came into better hands, as I soon after did; for our good father being shortly after chosen head, or, as they stile it, guardian of another convent, about twenty-four miles from this, and in an archiepiscopal city, where was also a college of Jesuits for the education of youth, he easily prevailed upon my mother to let me go with him thither, and to board at the monastery under his eye, whilst I went on with my studies at the college, where he also promised to recommend me to the care of those fathers. He likewise promised her that he would, in the evening, make me repeat and explain what I had learned in the day, and by that means push me so forward in my learning that I should out-top all my age, all which proved such powerful persuasives to my mother, that she easily agreed to it, especially as he took four or five more youths with him to be on the same foot with me both at the college and in the convent. We set out accordingly with him for the place, and when I was introduced into the Jesuits college, there was no small strife what class I should be admitted into at first. Here it will be necessary to acquaint the reader that the Jesuits distinguish their forms, or, as they more properly stile them, classes, each of them being kept in a separate apartment, as follows, viz.

1. The vith, or lowest, where they begin to learn the Latin Grammar.
2. vth, where they perfect themselves in that, and begin to learn some Latin books, and to make some wretched Latin.
3. ivth, where they read Tacitus, Cicero's Epistles, Ovid, and some other easy Roman authors, and begin to make better Latin.

4. iiid, where they read Curtius, Cicero's speeches, Virgil, and make pretty good Latin, and learn to make Latin verses. They likewise begin here to learn the Greek Grammar.

5. Humanity. In this class they read Horace, Cicero, Terence, make good verses, and compose some set speeches on a subject given, and if they have a genius for it, make some considerable progress in the Greek tongue, though they only read homilies of the fathers, and make versions out of Latin into Greek. They likewise make some set speeches, or poetical works, before a full audience.

6. Rhetoric. Here Homer and other Greek poets, Demosthenes and other Greek authors, are read; together with Cicero de Oratore, Horace's Satyres, and de Arte poetica. Themes are composed on given subjects, as much as can be, in the Ciceronian stile and method; and likewise poems in imitation of the Greek and Latin poets, and other books, compiled by some of the society for the use of this class, as there are others for every class else, and every branch of learning that is taught in them, the greatest part of which is to be learned by heart by the scholars, as well as several other persons, out of the classic authors, in order to exercise their memory, as is pretended, but rather serves to clog it with a deal of unintelligible stuff, which being sooner forgot than learned, serves to little purpose, except it be to take up so much of their time, to the neglect of more useful things, and more adapted to their capacities; to which I may safely add another great inconveniency, viz. that these lessons being to be repeated to the decurions or monitors, before the regent comes in, and an account to be given to him who hath, or who hath not learned them duely, in order to be commended or reproved, both the scholar and the monitor are in such haste to go through the drudgery, that those are

most approved of who can repeat theirs with the greatest speed, or rather with precipitation, by which such an habit is formed of speaking and reading with such monstrous quickness, as will require a great deal of trouble and pains, to break one's self off afterwards, if ever it is really rectified, and this I found long since to my loss, and no small grief.

7. The last is philosophy, which they divide into logic, physics, metaphysics, and morality, each of which takes them a quarter of a year in learning, or, at least, in expounding. Every scholar is obliged to spend a year at least in each of the classes; and if, at the year's end, when they are all to be separately examined, any be found tardy, either through dulness or negligence, they are condemned to go through the same studies another year, whilst the rest, who are found worthy, are promoted to the next class in rank.

When I came therefore to be acquainted with the particular studies and books of each class, and came to reflect on my being such a stranger to the classics, I begged of my old master that I might be offered only as candidate for the third class, where they began to be taught, and this I should have looked upon as a favour, considering that it was then Midsummer, and that I was herded as a beginner into a class where the rest had already studied six months; so that I thought I should have still enough to do to overtake them before the year was out. But the good father would by no means agree to it, but insisted upon my being examined as a candidate to humanity. This, I complained, was putting a double hardship upon me, being an utter stranger to the every author that was read in this as well as in the other below it, and having, at most, but seven months to master them all; he so far engaged, though against my will, for my overcoming all those difficulties by my genius and application, that I was obliged to undergo the examination of a candidate for humanity: and though my repugnance made me less solicitous how I went through it, as I was so desirous to be sent down to the class below it, yet whether the old monk's interest prevailed, or my own merit gained it, I was readily admitted into the class of humanity, and found it a very hard tug to keep up my credit under those disadvantages I laboured under. I wondered indeed how my old master could be guilty of such a neglect, and often pressed him to give me his assistance, which he trying to comply with, gave me but too fair an opportunity of discovering the true cause of it, viz. his being as unacquainted with them as I was. This therefore proved a very difficult class to me; and what was still more discouraging to me was, that our regent, so they call the person that teaches in every class, instead of making any kind allowance for my tender years, for my being entered so late, and under such disadvantages, often charged me with neglect and indolence, and, in a jocose manner, threatened to leave me inter manentes, that is, instead of raising to the next class, to leave me in this for another year. And though I was sensible that would have been more for my advantage, yet the shame of it was what I could not have brooked; and I thought it a mortification more than sufficient to be ranked among the middlemost of his class, who had till then been used to be at the head. But this he did rather to spur me on than to dispirit me, that I might the more easily be admitted into the class of rhetoric against the time of the yearly examination. This grand ceremony is performed a little before the Christmas holidays, and when the scholars have learned their doom, that is, whether to go up or to stay in the old class, they break up for ten or twelve days, and go to their respective homes. There were at this time four or five of my own townsboys, all of them not only much older, but who had been at the college several years before me, and bore a kind of envy against me for being admitted at once into the same class with them, and would have been glad to have left me behind in it. This consideration, joined to the displeasure such a piece of news would have been, not only to my old master, but much more so to my mother, made me so much the more diligent against the time of trial, and the more easily forego the advantage of another year's humanity: for the pride and pleasure of keeping pace with, and following them into rhetoric. Accordingly, I exerted myself so well, and gave such satisfaction at my examination, that I was nominated, as well as they, for that higher class. But tho' this gave me no small joy, and made me go home with a lighter heart, yet I have had since sufficient reason to wish it had proved otherwise; for our next regent, (the Jesuits customs is to change them every year, and to send new ones out of other colleges) proved a person every way almost unqualified for that high class, so that we rather went backwards than forward under him. He essayed at first to expound some of the Greek poets and orators by the help of the Latin versions annexed to them, in doing which he so far betrayed his ignorance of that tongue, that every one of us soon became sensible of it, which obliged him to set it quite aside. He was not much happier in the Latin ones, though better acquainted with them, and took at length such a disgust to the college method, that he may justly be said to have diverted himself with teaching us things quite opposite to it, and altogether foreign to our class, but which suited his genius better.

It will not be amiss to observe here, that the three main qualifications that procure admission into that society, are quality, or high rank, learning and riches. Our good regent was one of the last sort, being the son of an overgrown citizen or tradesman, who brought money enough into the fraternity to make amends for his want of learning; and as this college was but an obscure one, in comparison to those which they have in their great universities, he might be thought perhaps good enough to teach here; at least, if he was not fit to do so here, he could be much less so any where else. He complied however so far with the rules of the college, and of our class, as to oblige us now and then to make verses, themes, versions, and such low exercises; but I soon found that he did not give himself the trouble of looking them over, or even, for form's sake, of commending or discommending our performances according to their merit. As he was of a facetious temper, he would often so far indulge his vein, as to entertain us for a whole hour with stories, which were neither calculated to improve our minds, nor to make us in love with our books. At length, quite tired, as he seemed, with the drudgery of the college, he took it into his head to teach us heraldry, geography, and fortification, instead of the proper lessons of our class; so that we were forced, in some measure, to exchange books for maps, coats of arms, plans of cities, castles, &c. and, at length, to dabble with him in clay and dirt, in order to make a variety of fortifications, with all their appurtenances and proper colours; and these he took no small pride in shewing to strangers, but with this salvo, that this was our and his employment only between the school hours, tho' we were but too sensible that they took up likewise all our school-time, so that some days we did nothing else but that, to the neglect of every other branch of learning that was proper for our class. At length, after having trifled away near two thirds of the year, to our no small detriment, and to my great regret, who was so far behind-hand in my my learning, I was timely relieved, as I thought, by a letter from my mother, informing me, that the rector of a small convent of Dominicans in our neighbourhood, was going to teach philosophy to as many young gentlemen as he could get, and inviting me to make one of the number.

I readily agreed to it, the convent being but a pleasant walk out of my native city; and though I found I must take my leave of the classics if I went, yet I thought the learning of philosophy would be both more creditable and useful, than the poor stuff which our Jesuit taught us; though had I been then as well acquainted with the subtleties of Tho. Aquinas (or rather Aristotle, for that is the philosophy which the Dominicans teach) as I became afterwards, I doubt whether I should ever have been one of his disciples, at least by my consent. However, I left the college without any further ceremony, and having acquainted four or five of our class that were my townsboys with my design, they soon followed me, and at our coming to the rector, we found that he had already about twenty more, some, from a great university about sixty miles off, others, from the neighbouring towns, several of them mere dunces and rustics, with no other education than a little smattering of the Latin tongue, and not above five or six tolerably qualified for the study we were engaging in. As for me, whatever my old Franciscan master might depend upon as to the strength of my genius and closeness of application, for acquiring these branches of learning I was still wanting in, yet the discouragements which I had already encountered through his mismanagement, in placing me in too high a form, as well as the time we had trifled away in the class of rhetoric, had much abated my thirst after learning; and the much greater disappointment I met with under this new pretended teacher of philosophy, quite compleated my misfortune, by turning it into a downright carelessness and indifference about it. For tho' I was naturally quick enough, and assiduous at whatever I could gain the mastery of, and applause for so doing, yet, whenever the case proved otherwise, no youth could be more naturally lazy and supine than I; so that I cannot but think, on the strictest recollection I can make, that these many discouragements so closely following one another, were rather the cause of that deplorable indolence I since contracted for all laudable application to study, than my own natural temper and genius, which, had it been rightly directed and encouraged by proper motives, and especially if kept under some strict discipline, might have easily been enabled to have overcome the greatest difficulties in almost every branch of learning: but to return to our Dominican rector.

He began as usual with logic, and displayed a pretty good talent at explaining it to as many of us as had a genius for it; for as to the rest, which were near two-thirds of his school, both he and we could easily perceive that he was only wronging them of their time and money, though little did I think how soon that was to be my case: for though I took his logic with such surprising quickness and delight, as to have but one competitor, and was become a great favourite of his, by the free and humorous way in which I used to put, now and then, some puzzling questions to him; yet when we came to the second branch, which was Aristotle's physics, with Aquinas's comments, I found it such an unintelligible jargon, and him so little qualified to explain it to us, that I became quite tired with it; for some of us, especially my competitor and I, expected at least that he would have made every point as clear and evident to us, as he had before in logical lectures, and have answered such objections as we were able to raise against either the doctrines, or his expositions; but, to our great surprize, we found that he had undertaken to expound what himself did not understand, and that Aquinas's subtilities and distinctions were as much above his reach as above ours. Thus, for instance, Aristotle's account of the materia prima, together with his subtile commentator's expositions on it, in which our rector spent above a fortnight, including the rubs we threw into his way, appeared to us such an unintelligible heap of stuff, that, at our taking leave of it, to pass to another point, we made ourselves very merry about it, and owned ourselves as much in the dark as when he began it; insomuch, that he was forced to own he never could thoroughly comprehend it, and only delivered it to us on the authority of that philosopher, and of his many eminent disciples of the Dominican order, such as Albertus Magnus, Aquinas, &c. &c. I have since, upon running over his lessons more carefully, found reason to doubt whether a much abler head than his, would not have been as much at a loss to have beat it into any man's brain, that would not be satisfied with words without a meaning. However, as I plainly perceived that his chief view was to get our money, without troubling himself whether our progress was answerable, I contracted by degrees such a habit of indolence and listlessness to all he said (especially as he had got a singular knack at extricating himself, when closely pressed, by some facetious joke or merry story) that I wrote his lectures, and heard his expositions, without any attention, or offering any objection, unless it was in the jocund way, and to enliven our drooping spirits, and without troubling myself whether what he said or answered was right or wrong.

I know not whether it was not owing to his perceiving this listlessness in us, that he began to raise our expectation and hopes that his metaphysics, which was soon to follow, would prove more delightful to us. We did indeed expect it, from the nature of the subjects it treats of, and were not a little impatient to have this quarter finished, that we might enter into a more entertaining field: but when we found ourselves no less disappointed in this, it only damped our spirits the more, and gave me a still greater dislike to the jargon of the school, so that by that time we entered into the last quarter, when ethics were to be the new subject of his lectures, and might have otherwise proved more useful and entertaining to us, if it had been handled by a more proper person, we were grown so tired and out of conceit with him, that we reaped no more benefit from it than we had from the rest; and instead of diverting ourselves with repetitions and disputes about his lessons, as we used to do at first, we studied to forget every subject he had discussed to us, as soon as we were got out of his sight. Thus having murdered, as I may say, another year, we were dismissed, not without great applause and compliments to some of us, on account of our parts and proficiency. But if I may judge of the rest by myself, to whom he was always pleased to allow the first rank, I am sure his praises were ill bestowed as to any benefit we had reaped from his pains and ours: however, I was by that time become so great a favourite to him, that he afterwards left no means nor caresses untried to induce me to enter into their order, and I believe, in the mind I then was in, he might easily have prevailed, had not my mother strenuously opposed it. I was sensible of my deficiency in all the branches of learning I had hitherto gone through, by the misconduct of those under whom I had learned, and could easily see what dunces both my old Franciscan master and this Dominican rector were, though they passed for able men; and where could I better conceal my own defects and ignorance than under a monkish habit, which would, at least, give one the reputation of learning? But this I had taken care to conceal from her, partly out of pride, and partly to prevent her taking it to heart, and our rector had address enough to make her believe I was a prodigy, considering how young I still was, and to persuade her to send me to the next university, and to learn theology there, promising to give me such a recommendation to the Dominicans who taught it there, as well as the Jesuits, that no pains should be spared to make me shine in the world. She easily consented to it, and he gave me a certificate directed to the prior of their convent at that great city, testifying that I had gone thro' a course of philosophy, and was fit to be admitted a student in theology, to which he tacked some farther commendations; all which could be of no service to me, unless I resolved to go and learn under the Dominicans, for the Jesuits would hardly have admitted me to that class, before I had gone a new course through their philosophy. It had been, indeed, much better for me to have chosen the latter, considering the little proficiency I had made in it; but my pride, and the fear of disobliging my mother, determined me to the former, and I offered myself accordingly, and was readily admitted a student under two very reverend rectors, the one for the morning, and the other for the afternoon; both very grave and learned, indeed, in their way; but, upon my first admittance, the school appeared to me like a new world, where I was looked upon as a little raw stripling, too young quite, in all appearance, to herd among the rest of the students, some of whom were twice my age, and none by many years so young as I. What was still more discouraging was, that here was no distinction made between those who had already studied near two years (for the whole course of theology lasts two whole years) and those who were but newly admitted. The same lectures were read and expounded to all alike, and in the usual course, so that those who came not at the very beginning, had no other chance, but at the end, to put middle and both ends together as well as they could, which made the old standers assume such an overbearing air over the new ones, as was altogether mortifying, at least it proved so to me, who never had, till then, seen my school-fellows so much above me.

I may fairly date the completion of my ruin from the time of my coming to this populous place, on more accounts than one: for first, the city was a noble, great one, full of gentry and nobility, of coaches, and all kinds of grandeur, all which did greatly affect me, who had never seen so much by far of the beau monde, neither in my native city, nor in the archiepiscopal one, where I had studied under the Jesuits. 2dly, I had been already cloyed with Aquinas's philosophy, when I had no such bright tempting objects dancing before my eyes, what likelihood could there be that such a school as this, should reconcile me to the more refined and unintelligible subtilities of his theology, especially considering the disadvantages we late comers were forced to labour under, and the high state which our two rectors took upon them? for here was no room for objecting, or even desiring a point or a term to be explained, and we had nothing to do but to write what they dictated, and take their expositions for sound doctrine. Even those who had studied longest under them, and were looked upon as the brightest, were not indulged to start a difficulty, though the occasion was ever so fair; all which damped my spirits, who had never been used to such a restraint, and had, moreover, the mortification to see myself placed in the lowest rank, who had, till then, been mostly at the head, that I grew by degrees quite out of conceit both with myself and with the school. What added still more to my discontentedness was, that I boarded at some near relations in one of the suburbs of the city, and at a great distance from the convent, and these commonly dined so late, that I must either take up with an irregular meal, or come near an hour after the rest to the school. I did indeed prefer the first for some time, but grew by degrees weary of it, as the study I was upon grew less engaging to me; so that though I took up as little time as I could at my dinner, yet one half hour, at least, was lost by it, and our rector had dictated some pages of matter to the rest, which, after school was over, I used to copy out of the manuscripts of some of my school-fellows. Our rector having more than once observed what irregular hours I kept, was so kind as to give me a civil reprimand, and not expecting, perhaps, a reply to it, was going on with his lecture, but I had been so little used to make answers to it in dumb show, as I observed many of his hearers were forced to do, that I bluntly told him the occasion, assuring him, that I had not influence enough in the family to prevail on them to alter their hours.

The good father not approving of my excuse, which plainly shewed that I could not forego my dinner for his lessons, and might be an ill precedent to some of the rest, seemed rather inclined to lay the fault on my being better pleased with those late hours of dining, or else he thought I might easily persuade my relations to alter their method on my account. But whether so or not, he insisted, and reasonably enough, that I should conform to the school-hours, whatever inconveniency it might put me as to my dinner. I was sensible of the justness of his reproof, and after having been often at high words with my relations (for they were fully paid for my board) to no purpose, and tried to conform to the school-hours for some time, I grew weary of it, and having nobody to controul me, which proved my greatest misfortune, I quite forsook the afternoon lectures, and spent that time in sauntring about the city and country adjacent, viewing the buildings, and sometimes taking plans and vistoes of such places as pleased me, but without any other design than to divert myself. I was, however, surprised soon after, to find myself interrogated by our morning professor, about the reason of my not coming to the afternoon lectures. Whether my quondam master of philosophy had wrote any thing particularly concerning his expectation of getting me into their order or not, I knew not, but I was in a genteel manner given to understand by this, that I ought to look on it as a singular favour that they so far concerned themselves about me. What answer I made him, besides my thanking him for his care, I cannot recollect; but though we parted good friends, I soon after forsook his lecture also, and from that time minded little else but my own pleasures, which, though altogether of the innocent kind, sometimes with the fair sex, at other times in viewing the curiosities of the place, or making solitary excursions, and the like; yet were not without some pungent remorse, as they tended to little else but to inure me to a habit of indolence and careless inactivity. At some intervals, indeed, I tried to read over all my manuscripts both in philosophy and theology, but still so disgusted with them, that I never had the patience to go through them.

I had before this sent some complaining letters to my mother, as well as messages by word of mouth by some of my townsmen, who had been witnesses of the bad hours we kept, and to whom I had related the inconveniency it had put to, with relation to my studies; and she, good woman, thinking that I took it more to heart than I did, sent me a small supply to convey me to Avignon, where I was to meet an old rich counsellor of our town, who was gone to spend some time in that famed city. He had no children of his own, but some nephews, one of which he designed to breed up a scholar under me, in consideration of which I was to lodge and board with the uncle, till I could better provide for myself. As this was likely to be a kind of change for the better for me, as well as an easement to my mother, whose strait circumstances could hardly permit her to be at such expence for my education, I made no delay to go down to Avignon, where I found the old gentleman ready to receive me, and, a day or two after, entered into my new office of tutor to his nephew, who had already made some progress in the Latin Grammar. I had not been long there before I got acquainted with a young abbé, or candidate for priestly orders, a countryman of mine, and an ingenious young man, of some learning; and he finding that I had studied philosophy and theology under the Dominicans, introduced me to one of their professors in this city, by whom I was courteously received, and soon after admitted to be one of his disciples. This father, who was a man of singular modesty and humanity, and was reputed a saint, paid me an uncommon regard upon my first admission to his lectures, and made an apology to the rest of his scholars for recapitulating some of his former lessons and expositions, *in gratiam*, as he was pleased to word it, *charissimi nostri novi discipuli*, that I might the better understand what he was then, and afterwards, to deliver to us. This great condescension, which had not been shewed to me by either of the professors of the last university, and which I since understood was not usual among them, did highly oblige me, and I would have been glad to have made such a proficiency under him, as might have, in some measure, answered his singular kindness to me, which he still continued to express all the time I went to hear him, but my misfortune was, that I was still so unacquainted as well as disgusted at the subtilities of the school, and met with such crampt distinctions and technical terms I was still a stranger to, and was ashamed to ask the meaning of from any of the scholars, who were far enough from thinking me so great a novice to the language of the Thomists, that I began again, in spite of all his caresses, and my own eager desires, to despair of ever becoming a theologian; and these difficulties added to the lazy and unthinking habit I had so long indulged, made me at length forbear going any more to hear him.

I have already hinted that my mother's circumstances were too narrow for the expence I had already put her to, and my father was still more unable to give her any assistance in it, though he was not a little pleased at the great progress he was told I had made for my years. Her hopes and mine were, indeed, that I might by that means introduce myself as a tutor into some good family, and save her all farther charges. But I had been so far neglected in the other parts of my education, had so little address or politeness, and knew so little of the world, that I could not look upon myself as fit for such an employment among persons above the common rank, and my pride would not let me aim at any thing below it; so that instead of trying as I might, and ought to have done, I was rather become careless and indifferent about it, and I was indeed both too young and too naturally unfit for it. Notwithstanding which, some of my acquaintance, unknown or undesired, got me into a middling family, where I was upon somewhat better terms than with my old counsellor; but the overgrown youth, who was put under my care, and was much older, and taller by the head and shoulders than I, had, by that time, contracted such an indolence, or rather averseness, both to the Latin tongue, and to other laudable studies, that had I been ever so diligent in teaching him, it would have been to little purpose, because, as I soon found, he wanted parts as well as inclination for study; so that we spent more of our time in playing on the violin and flute than at our books. His mother, who heard us at it longer and oftner than she thought was consistent with the progress she expected him to make under me, complained more than once of it to me; upon which I made no difficulty to tell her, that a greater degree of application would rather confirm him in his averseness, than reconcile him to his study, as he had so small a capacity for it. I left this soon after for a better place with a person of distinction, who intrusted two sons of his to my care, both very young, and spoiled by the mother, that the eldest, above seven years of age, could but just read, and neither of them inclined to learn. I tried what I could to bring them to it, but to little purpose, except a little history, which the eldest took more freely to, but the mother's indulgence was not the only obstacle, and as she was a sprightly lady, and her spouse somewhat heavy, though not old, I soon found by her behaviour, and her parting beds with him soon after my coming, that she would have been better pleased I had transferred my care from them to her; and as I was naturally fond of ingratiating myself with the sex, I indulged her in all her little foibles, but without having the least design of going farther than a bare complaisance, in order to gain her esteem and admiration, rather than her affection, and to satisfy my own vanity, rather than cherish a dangerous passion for her. This made me to take frequent occasions to recommend myself by false merit, since I had no real one that could do it, by pretending to more virtue and religion than I had, and to palliate the low circumstances of my parents by some vain excuses, and pretences, all which I did with so little caution, and in so aukward a manner, as made me appear rather more despicable in her eyes, considering the mean appearance I made, and which was owing chiefly to my own negligence and bad economy.

All these disadvantages, however, might have been easily overlooked, and I might have been readily suffered to indulge my own prevailing passion, if I could but have shewed more concern for hers.

It is not my design to dwell on such scenes as these, much less to ascribe my neglect and overlooking the several distant offers made by so agreeable a person to my own virtue. I might more justly impute it to my natural sheepish bashfulness, and unexperienced youth; however, after a six month's stay, and some visible proofs that it was not in my power to conquer it, I perceived a strange coldness to succeed, which made me think it would not be long before I was discharged. She was soon after visited by some relations, who persuaded her to go and spend some part of the summer with them about twenty miles off. They, especially the gentlemen, affected the air of libertines, and all of them expressed a singular contempt for the superstitions of the church of Rome, by which I guessed them to be concealed Protestants, of whom there were great numbers in Languedoc, Provence, Dauphinee, and I have had since reason to think, that my young lady was so likewise, by her light behaviour at church, and on other occasions. I had some small disputes with them, being then very zealous for that church, but they knowing that I had studied divinity, and fearing, I suppose, lest too eager an opposition to what I urged against them should cause a discovery, they declined entering the list with me any farther, and I then found, for the first time, that the Protestants had more to say for themselves than I had ever imagined; for the divinity we were taught at the schools seldom meddled with the controversies between us and the Protestants, so that had it not been for fear, those gentlemen, I found, might easily have foiled me, notwithstanding all my theology. The lady was preparing for her journey, and was to take her sons with her, yet kept me in suspense whether I was to accompany her, or stay with her husband, or be discharged. I have had reason to think since, that she had an end in it; but finding my behaviour still aukward and unpromising, notwithstanding some fresh essays, which I did not then so well comprehend, she left it to her husband, who was a person that cared for nothing but his bottle, and left her to do as she pleased in every thing else, to acquaint me with the news that they should have no farther occasion for me. I was more grieved than surprised at it, which, she perceiving, occasioned one more snare to be laid by means of the chambermaid, which proving still unsuccessful, and this was the very night before they were to set out, I was despised and laughed at, and given to understand, that I might thank myself if the lady and I went different ways.

I have already hinted that virtue and religion had little or no share in my disappointing her, but rather a vanity of being thought more chaste than I really was, which kept me so indeed, as to the act, not only on this, but many other rencounters, though in heart and thought few men were more strangers to that virtue than I, even at those tender years; and though religion, which, in all my foolish extravagancies, I never once lost sight of, held still some check on my mind, yet it could hardly turn even the scale against any favourite passion of mine, farther than to make me condemn myself after having yielded to it; so that it was rather the fear of a repulse, or some other or worse consequence that kept me from shewing an equal ardor for her, whatever opinion my different behaviour might give her of me. The company and she were no sooner gone than I took the road to Avignon, where I heard that my old counsellor was gone home, with his nephews, to my no small grief, especially as my pockets were then low; the widow where we had boarded very poor, and I had so few acquaintance in that city; however, I ventured to stay with her till I could write to my mother for a fresh supply, or till something better fell in my way, though I had little reason to expect any success from either; being by this time become very shabby in cloaths and linnen, and more indolent and inactive than ever. To ward off, as much as possible, the pungent mortification of my present circumstances, I had recourse to my old stratagem, of cloathing myself with some false merit for want of a great one, and of pretending to be a sufferer for religion for a too great attachment to the church, and laying most of the blame on my own father, as using me the more severely on that account; all which, though abominably false in every respect, yet being too easily listened to by some of my acquaintance, especially among the friars, did gain me so much pity and admiration, as soothed my vanity for the present, though it did not answer the main end I proposed, its introducing me into some new family as a tutor, and at the same time accounting, in some tolerable measure, for the mean appearance I then made.

I was about the same time informed that the famed fair of Baucaire, a city in Languedoc, on the Rhone, and one of the largest fairs in Europe, was at hand, and that among the great concourse at it, I might meet with some of my own townsmen, from whom I might get a fresh supply. I went accordingly, and found there several merchants of my acquaintance, who furnished me with as much money for the present, as would just serve, but, on the next day, when I expected to have received a much larger sum, I only met with a severe reprimand for my mean appearance, and for not having made a better use of the opportunities I had had of discharging my mother from all future expences on my account. I excused it as well as I could to them, they being no strangers to the great poverty, not to say universal misery, that then reigned at Avignon, where the streets abounded with people, who, from living very comfortably, and some of them richly, on the silk manufacture of the place, were, on the decay of it, reduced to the lowest degree of beggary. They told me, that though that was too truly the case of the tradesmen, yet the priests and monks lived in as much plenty as ever, and a lad of my parts and learning might easily have found means to have recommended himself to some of them, instead of appearing in such a guise as I did, and which they said made them apprehensive I had taken up some ill courses. This censure, which was no less unjust than severe, if they spoke what they thought, did cut me to the heart; for no youth could be more free from the vices of drinking, gaming, intriguing, &c. than I was. Happy it would have been for me if I could have as easily disculpated myself from those of indolence, vanity, and bad oeconomy; for these were the true sources of my misfortunes, insomuch that I am persuaded, if they had supplied me with as great a sum, as I could in reason have desired, I should have been induced to have laid out the greatest part of it in such curious nicknacks and trifles as that fair affords, especially of the musical kind; for I had already, in that short interval, agreed for a good number of them; but whether they had set any body to watch my motions, and guessed at the preposterous use I should make of what money they might lend me, or whatever other reason they might have, they absolutely refused to let me have even so much as would bring me back to Avignon; so that one may easily imagine the dismal plight I was in all the way thither, to say nothing of that mortification I should meet with among my acquaintance there at my ill success. I found, however, a plausible excuse for it, by pretending that I was come a day or two too late, and that the merchants were, by that time, so short of cash that they could not supply me, but that they would remit me what I wanted soon after their return home. I likewise told my old landlady, to whom I was hardly indebted for a quarter of a year's board and lodging, that I expected two of them to be there shortly at an approaching fair, which was actually true, and she knew and dealt with one of them for some sort of goods, so that had I had the patience to have staid till then, my mother, who had expressed no small resentment at their ungenerous refusal, would not have failed sending me a fresh supply by them; whereas, hearing that I had left the place, she sent only what would pay the poor woman, whilst I, unknown to her, or any one else, had taken a resolution to return home, bare as I was of money and cloaths.

I lately took notice of my shameful pretence of being a kind of sufferer for religion, to some of my acquaintance, and tho' vanity and my then ill plight was my only incentive to it, I began now to think it might be made a means of facilitating my long journey homewards; I went accordingly and furnished myself with a kind of pass, or certificate, at a proper office, signifying that I was a young student in theology, of Irish extract, and that I had left the country for the sake of religion, by which is commonly implied the Roman Catholic, and that I was then going on a pilgrimage to Rome. This absurd and false assertion cost me since many a shameful lye to make it pass for current, especially as often as I met with any persons who had any tolerable knowledge of Irish affairs, to which I was an utter stranger. I did, indeed, know several English and Irish, who had followed king James's fortune, and were well respected in France, Italy, &c. but my vanity could not be satisfied with the credit of passing for the son of some one of them; I wanted to have it thought my own voluntary act, that I forsook that country and my parents, and fortune, for the sake of religion. Had the secretary, from whom I had procured that certificate, been ever so little diffident, my very name, which had nothing of Irish or English, but which my pride would not let me forego, because it had something of quality in it, would easily have discovered the roguery of the pretence; and this I mention to shew my rashness and ignorance, of which I shall give a further instance, in the method I took immediately after obtaining the pass, to equip myself in a pilgrim's garb; for I was not in a condition to purchase one, tho' it consisted only of a long staff handsomely turned, and a short leathern or oil-cloth cloak, not unlike what the women call a pelerine. However, I had observed such a one in a chapel belonging to a parish-church, and dedicated to a miraculous saint, which, I suppose, had been set up there as a monument of gratitude by some wandering pilgrim come to the end of his journey. The chapel was never without a number of devotees, who prayed and burnt tapers before the image of the saint; but this did not deter me from venturing in, and taking both staff and cloak away at noon-day; had I been examined about it, I was only furnished with a juvenile pretence, that I looked upon it to be set up there to accommodate such pilgrims as could not otherwise provide themselves with it. How far such a poor excuse might have gone I know not, neither did I trouble my head about it; however, I escaped without such an enquiry, and carried it off unmolested, and made what haste I could to some private corner, where I threw the cloak over my shoulders, and walked with a sanctified gravity with the staff in my hand, till I was got out of the city.

Being thus accoutred, and furnished with a pass to my mind, I began at all proper places to beg my way in a fluent Latin; accosting only clergymen, or persons of figure, by whom I could be understood, and was most likely to be relieved; and I found them mostly so generous and credulous, that had I had the least propensity to provide for hereafter, I might easily have saved a good deal of money, and put myself into a much more creditable garb, before I had gone through a score or two of miles; but such was my vanity and extravagance, that as soon as I had got what I thought a sufficient viaticum, I begged no more, but viewed every thing worth seeing, then retired to some inn, where I spent my money as freely as I got it, not without some such aukward tokens of generosity, as better suited with my vanity than my present circumstances. The nearer I drew to my native place, the more irresolute I grew, whether I should pay a visit to my mother, or continue my journey to Rome; the concern I knew she must be in about me, strongly inclined me to the former, but my uncommon mean garb, which was become only more scandalous by the length of the journey, made me so ashamed to be seen either by her, or any of my friends, that I fully resolved on the latter. I had, in order to it, wheeled about to the left, to leave the place at some twenty or thirty miles distance, and was got into a small town where I little expected to be known, when venturing on the Sunday into the church, at the time of high mass, I was surprised to see some persons, especially two or three gentlewomen, whose chief residence was at my native city, but who it seems were spending part of the summer at that place, and who, in spight of my being thus transmogrified, did easily recall me to mind, and gave me to understand they did. I was so shocked at it, that I left the church at the most solemn part of the service, when they were most intent on their devotions, not caring to stand an examen from them, and made the best of

75

my way through private paths, to avoid being caught if pursued. Whether I was so I know not, but the sight of them made such a strong impression on my mind, and raised such an earnest desire in me of seeing once more that beloved city, especially considering that it was now impossible to conceal either my way of travelling, or mean appearance from my friends, that as soon as I thought myself out of the reach of a pursuit, I took the direct road homeward, with an intent to go and satisfy my poor anxious mother, before she got the intelligence from other hands, and consult with her, whether I should pursue my journey to Rome, or get into any other way she liked better. And I only took care to enter the city in the dusk of the evening, and got to her house unperceived by any but those of the family.

My poor mother was glad to see me, tho' sorry to behold the mean garb I was in, and failed not, though with her usual tenderness, to chide me, for having made so bad an use of the opportunities, she supposed I had had, of pushing my fortune, which, she knew as well as I, was but too much owing to my indolence. Much more reason would she have had to chide me, had she known how much of my time I had trifled away during the last year and half I had been absent from her; but that I concealed from her, and the good woman was sometimes inclined to think, that my too great eagerness after my studies had made me neglect every thing else. But I was greatly surprised at the end of two or three days, during which I had kept as much from sight as I could, to hear her propose to me, since I had found out so cheap, safe, and easy a way of travelling, to go and pay a visit to my father, who then lived some hundreds of miles from her, and try what I could get him to do for me; and I had the more reason to wonder at her proposal, because she knew, as well as I, that a tradesman of our town, who had been with him about two or three years before, had brought us a very indifferent account of his circumstances. This made me suspect that a cousin of mine, and a great favourite of hers, whose fortune was in no wise suitable to his high spirit, had put that strange project in her head, that I might be far enough out of the way of obstructing her kindness to him. Whether there was any real foundation for my suspicion, I cannot say, but the surprize she observed me to be in at her proposal, made such an impression upon her, that she forgot nothing that could assure me of her maternal and unalterable tenderness, alledging that she only wanted to be better satisfied of the condition my father was in, than she was from the report of the tradesman above mentioned, and adding, that in case I found it not to my liking, and him as tender as I might expect, she charged me expressly to leave him, and come back to her as soon as possible, and by no means to stay longer than a year from her, unless I could convince her that it was very much to my advantage.

Being thus far satisfied of her maternal affection, I easily consented to take the journey, having by that time contracted an inclination to ramble and see new countries, and as it was a long and dangerous one, we thought it improper to alter my dress, the meaness of which would rather be a safeguard; however, she thought fit to sew up a small quantity of gold to my cloaths, which, she said, would serve to buy me some better ones, when I came near the end of my journey. My staff and cloak, with the addition of a long loose gown, made of a light kind of black buckram to cover the rest from dust, were sent by a man to a place on the road, about four miles off; and very early in the morning I took a sorrowful leave of my mother, and she of me, and she repeated her charge to me to return to her, if I did not find things to my satisfaction. When I came to the place where my pilgrim's dress waited for me, I put it on, and went on not without a heavy heart, tho' without the least doubt of my mother's constant affection. My direct rout was thro' the first great university where I had began to study theology, so that I was forced to wheel about to avoid it, for fear of being known. All the rest of the way I was an utter stranger to, and I met frequently with some objects that made me shrink, tho' it was a considerable high road; now and then at some lonely place lay the carcase of a man rotting and stinking on the ground by the way-side, with a rope about his neck, which was fastened to a post about two or three yards distance, and these were the bodies of highwaymen, or rather of soldiers, sailors, mariners, or even galley-slaves, disbanded after the peace of Reswick, who, having neither home nor occupation, used to infest the roads in troops, plunder towns and villages, and when taken were hanged at the county-town by dozens, or even scores sometimes, after which their bodies were thus exposed along the highway *in terrorem*. At other places one met with crosses, either of wood or stone, the highest not above two or three feet, with inscriptions to this purport; "pray for the soul of A. B. or of a stranger that was found murdered on this spot." These deterring objects made me willing to associate myself to some fellow-travellers whom I met on the same road; but such was my vanity, that I never renewed the pilgrim's trade of begging whilst any of my money lasted, but was rather lavish of it on some of them, tho' I know not how soon I might feel the want of it; and I had not resumed it long before I met with such a mortification as made me heartily repent of my folly. I was to go through the celebrated city of Lyons, abounding with the finest buildings and other curiosities, which I was very desirous to see; and when I came to one of the gates, was asked by an officer, in a livery like our beadles, whether I wanted a viaticum? Not knowing the consequence of his question, I answered in the affirmative, and was bid immediately to follow him. I was surprised at the length of the way he led me, and observed several fine churches, palaces, squares, &c. which I stood still to admire, but was not suffered to do so long; and at length, after about an hour and half's good walking, was told, that that was the opposite gate at which I was to go out and pursue my journey; he then clapped a couple of pence into my hand, and told me, that I must not venture back into the city under some severe punishment, and left me quite astonished and unable to reply. As soon as I had recovered myself, I began to reflect on my extravagance and disappointment in a most lively manner, but thought it best, however, to follow his advice, rather than expose myself to some shameful treatment, if I attempted to return. What increased my concern was, the fear of finding the same method observed in every great city I came to, but, happily for me, it proved otherwise, and I not only went through them all without molestation, but staid in some of them long enough to view every thing worth seeing, and to converse with men of learning and piety, from whom I received some tokens of their generosity.

The misfortune was, that my rashness and vanity would not suffer me to keep within due bounds, but I must set myself off to the highest advantage, by pretending to greater merit and learning than was consistent even with common prudence, as it exposed me to the continual danger of a shameful discovery. I took notice heretofore how little progress I had made in the Greek tongue, rather through the ignorance and neglect of some of my teachers, than want of capacity or application, but now I pretended to be not only master of it, but likewise in some measure of the Hebrew, though I knew not a single letter of the latter, and had only seen some Hebrew books belonging to the Jews of Avignon, by which I just could distinguish that from other characters; the truth is, that neither that nor any of the oriental tongues, nor even the Greek, were much studied by the clergy; so

I was not under any great danger on that account, though I own I have been sometimes foiled at the latter, because I commonly addressed myself to the priests, among whom I met, now and then, with one who understood it. I must also acknowledge that I found the generality of them very charitable, and some of them even generous, though it the more redounds to my shame, seeing neither the meanness of my garb, of which yet I was not a little ashamed, nor the mortifying accidents that had happened to me could prevail upon me to save a shilling towards buying any thing better. I had indeed some hopes to do so, as I came nearer to my father, but here I was again justly disappointed; the two or three last provinces I was to pass through, having been greatly impoverished, and even laid waste by the late war, so that I found the clergy here less rich and generous, and so great poverty reigned among the laity, that I had much ado to get sufficient subsistance among them. I should likewise observe here, that every town, or even village I came through, had a number of Lutherans and Calvinists, who were still in a worse condition, insomuch that their ministers were obliged to keep some poor inn or alehouse for subsistance; so that by that time I had reached my father I was quite pennyless and threadbare. I presently, however, made myself known to him, though to his great surprise, not only on that account, but as it was such an unexpected visit, of which he had not had the least notice given him, nor did at all dream of. The city where I met him being about three or four miles from his house, he clapped a small piece in my hand, and directed me to a house where I might get some refreshment, and towards night conducted me to his own home, which I was not a little surprised to find even meaner than our townsman had described to my mother and me. Here he bid me a fresh and most tender welcome, and expressed such a visible concern that he was not able to give me at least as good entertainment as I had been used to with my mother, that I was hardly able to make him a proper answer.

And indeed the difference I found between the two places, the forlorn condition I saw myself in, the mean figure I made in an obscure kind of village, my being now not only out of the way of any improvement, but in danger of losing what I had got, afforded me such a dismal prospect, that I could not easily conceal my uneasiness, and, in a little time, a more than ordinary desire of returning to my old home, since this new one was in every respect so little inviting to me. He found it no less difficult to conceal his dislike of my returning to my mother, and tried all he could to dissuade me from it. He advised me to try my fortune at two or three neighbouring cities or universities, and I complied with his desire, but found much greater discouragements than I could expect: first, the Jesuits were the teachers in all of them, and I had studied with the Dominicans, between whom and them there never was a right understanding, but rather quite the contrary. I was got into a new country, (Germany) where the pronunciation of the Latin differed so much from that I had been used to, that though no one could speak it more fluently than I, I neither could understand them, nor make myself understood by them, without the greatest difficulty. The country had been so ruined by the war, that those few mendicant scholars that remained in those universities[1], might be rather said to starve than to subsist. My youth and ignorance of the

---

1    Most of the universities of Germany have a number of these mendicant students, who, as soon as the school hours are over, go along the streets from house to house, singing some pious Latin verses to sex cite people's charity, and in some opulent cities, get enough to live well and comfortably, and to buy all the books that are necessary for them, by which means some of them become very learned men, and get to good prefer- ment, but as it was quite otherwise in these, and, indeed, every city along the Rhine, quite down below the great city of Cologn (where the French forces had caused such dreadful delapidations as could not be seen without horror), these universities had been long since forsaken by all those mendicant students, who could no longer find means of subsisting them. And this I afterwards observed to be the case in every place where the French troops had been, as I may have further occasion to show in the sequel.

German tongue, as well as my foreign pronunciation of the Latin and Greek, would likewise have disqualified me for being a tutor in any family, had there been any in a condition to have maintained one; so that after all my efforts, which I rather tried out of obedience to my father, than any likely hopes I could have of success, I returned to him re infecta, all which only served to revive my desires of returning to my mother. But he being still as averse to it as ever, bethought himself of a new way to dissuade me from it, and with so much art at the same time, that I could not discover his aim. He had seen the greatest part of Europe, and could give an extraordinary account of it; he understood several of its languages, particularly the Italian, French, Spanish and German, and expatiated much on the advantages he had gained by travelling; and expressed, at some distance, a desire that I should visit several of those countries I had not yet seen, particularly those of Holland, Flanders, and Brabant, which he highly commended for their opulence, and the great number of learned men they produced, and expatiated much on their hospitality, generosity, and fondness for men of parts and genius, and how greatly I might be admired and promoted there on account of my learning, knowledge of languages and sciences, and for having already travelled through so many considerable parts of the world, all which he said was the more surprising, as I was still so very young, for I was then hardly full sixteen years old. He could not indeed have found a more effectual way than that of soothing my vanity, to make me give wholly into his views, and as to the objection of the want of money, considering how well acquainted I was with the way of travelling at free-cost, he said I could not but promise myself much better success through those countries, where the peoples generosity was equal to their known opulence.

I was now (unknown to him) to think of some more cunning,

safe, and effectual way of travelling than that I had followed in my two former journies; and since I found that my passing for an Irishman and a sufferer for religion, did not only expose me to the danger of being discovered, but came short of the merit and admiration I had expected from it, I resolved on a new project, which, though equally hazardous, I had not sense enough to foresee, and tho' still more dishonest, I had not virtue enough to deter me from. I say, unknown to my father, for I had carefully concealed all the vile indirect pretences I had already used, and much more was I now obliged to do so, knowing him to be so upright and religious a man, that I should not only have incurred his utmost anger, but that he would likewise have taken all possible means to have deterred me from, or disappointed me in it. I recollected, that whilst I was learning humanity, rhetoric and geography with the Jesuits, I had heard them speak of the East-Indies, China, Japan, &c. and expatiate much in praise of those countries, and the ingenuity of the inhabitants. The idea they had given us of them was indeed too general and imperfect, at least what I remembered of it, was by far too short and confused, for a person of the least prudence or forecast to have built such a wild project upon, because all the notion they had given us of it, was only from their maps and comments upon them, for they made use of geographical books. However, I was rash enough to think, that what I wanted of a right knowledge of them, I might make up by the strength of a pregnant invention, in which I flattered myself I might succeed the more easily, as I supposed they were so little known by the generality of Europeans, that they were only looked upon, in the lump, to be Antipodes to them in almost every respect, as religion, manners, dress, &c. This was my crude notion of the matter, which I thought afforded a vast scope to a fertile fancy to work upon, and I had no mistrust of myself on that head. I had likewise heard that their way of writing differed very much from ours, but how, and in what, I was altogether ignorant, or had quite forgot it, and so took it into my head, that like the Hebrew, and other oriental tongues I had heard of, they must write from the right to the left, and on this puerile supposition, I set about excogitating of an alphabet that might answer my purpose. Another thing that shewed my inconsiderate folly was, that tho' I could not but know that the Greeks and Hebrews had particular names for their letters, it never came once into my head to imitate them in that, as I had in the figures, powers, &c. of some of the letters on a supposition, that as they might flow originally from the same fountain, so they might be reasonably imagined to retain still some kind of resemblance. The truth is, my time was short, and knowledge in what I went about so very small and confused, and what I did was by stealth, and fear of being detected by my father; that I was soon after made sensible of my want of forecast, when I came to converse with proper judges, and found the necessity not only of inventing names for the letters, but to make several amendments to my wild scheme, as I became better acquainted with those Eastern countries.

However, considering my tender years, small experience, and other such disadvantages, I have had since no small cause to wonder how I could excogitate not only such an alphabet, and names of letters, but likewise many other particulars equally difficult, such as a considerable piece of a new language and grammar, a new division of the year into twenty months, a new religion, &c. and all out of my own head, in order to stuff them into that most abominable romance which I published soon after my coming into England, and which occasioned such variety of opinions concerning it, and its shameless author; some thinking it above the capacity of such a young fellow to invent, and others believing it the result of long thought and contrivance. Alas, for me, my fancy was but too fertile and ready for all such things, when I set about them, and when any question has been started on a sudden, about matters I was ever so unprepared for, I seldom found myself at a loss for a quick answer, which, if satisfactory, I stored up in my retentive memory. But to return to my alphabet, as soon as I had finished it to my mind, I began to inure my hand to write it with some readiness, that it might upon occasion appear natural to me, which I found the more difficult, as I never was expert at my pen, and was quite unused to this backward way of writing; and this obliged me to alter the form of some of them, for the more easy tracing them with the pen, and to contrive some abreviations and joining of letters, and other such improvements for expedition, which done, I thought myself sufficiently prepared for passing for a Japanese converted to Christianity. The only difficulty was, how to reconcile this new and vile assumption with my Avignon certificate, which was not to be done but by copying it anew, and altering it where I saw fit, and clapping the seal from the original one to the counterfeit; but though I was ready enough at wording it to my mind, I wrote so indifferent a hand, that it could never pass for that of a secretary of a vice-legate, and to have had it done by a better penman was too difficult and hazardous for me to venture. At length I thought it safest to trust to my copying it as well as I could, with its flourishes and ornaments, though I did it in such a coarse and clumsy manner, that it would hardly have passed for a tolerable counterfeit. There was likewise another danger of a discovery from the different marks and make of the German and Avignon paper, but that never came then in my head; so that having made what alterations I thought proper in the tenor of the pass, and clapping the old seal to it, I made no difficulty to trust the rest to fortune, and took a melancholy leave of my poor father, who shed abundance of tears over me, and wished me all possible blessings and success, not dreaming how little this new project of mine deserved of either; and when I was got at some distance from him, I put on my old pilgrim's habit, and began my journey with a kind of heavy heart, according to the rout he had penned down for me, and which was quite opposite to that which would have brought me to my own home. I had, indeed, taken care to write to my anxious mother, and to acquaint her with what had passed between my father and me, and with my desire of taking a tour into the Low Countries before I returned to her, but I had afterwards reason to fear, that the melancholy style in which it was worded, did rather increase than mitigate her concern for her now really worthless son; for, from that time, neither she, nor yet my father, ever heard of me more, nor I of them, and, in all likelihood, both of them have bewailed my loss at a much greater rate than I deserved, if it did not prove the means of shortening their days.

The reader may see by all this, what a rash and abandoned fellow I was, how lost to all sense of religion, nature and reason, and how I exposed myself to so many dangers, over head and ears, to indulge a favourite passion, and without the least prospect of reaping any benefit from it, or even aiming at it. However, this is nothing in comparison of what is to follow, and it is rather a wonder that so bad a beginning, so ill concerted, and worse followed, hath not had a more dreadful ending, and I can only ascribe it to the undeserved mercy of God, that it did not end in my total ruin of body and soul. And I must desire the reader to bear still in mind the consideration of my tender years, and the disadvantages of my wrong education, if he intends to read what is to follow with any tolerable patience, at least till he comes to some more agreeable scenes: In the mean time, as I am now entering into One of the blackest shame and guilt, I sincerely protest, that it is the farthest from my heart to aggravate or extenuate either, in order to render the following account more surprizing or agreeable, but to relate the whole with the same sincerity, as I should be willing to do it, or wish it to have been done, at my last moments. And I hope I shall be the more readily believed, as I do not design to have it printed till after my death, when all sinister views will be quite taken away, and nothing be able to yield any satisfaction on the other side of the grave, but the consciousness of its sincerity, especially considering that I shall leave neither children nor relations to reap any benefit from this narrative. But to return to my proposed rout:

I was at first to visit all the considerable cities on both sides of the Rhine, as they lay in my way to that of Cologn, whither I pretended to go on a religious pilgrimage to the three kings, whose remains are said to be there interred in the cathedral[2], to which there is a great resort of devotees almost all the year: for the Germans are equally fond of pilgrims that come to any of their great saints, as the Italians are of those that come to Rome or Loretto, or the Spaniards to those that go to St. Jago de Compostella; so that I did not doubt of meeting with a kind reception wherever I came. I shall not take up the reader's time in describing the places I came through, that being much better done in books of travels; but only observe, that I found them all in a most dismal plight, most of the fine buildings ruinated, noble palaces with only the bare walls, half demolished, cathedrals, and other stately churches, built of the finest marble and other costly stones finely carved, battered half down, and nothing left fit for divine service but the choir or chancel, which in many

---

2   Those were the wise men who came to worship the Infant Saviour, and are, by the Church of Rome, stiled kings, and pretended to be only three, whom they call Gaspar, Melchior and Balthazar; the legend adds, that upon their being warned not to return to Jerusalem, they took toe way to Cologn, and died, and were buried there. Their heads are exposed in a stately shrine behind the great altar every Wednesday, and they shew you the gate by the Rhine-side, at which it is pretended they came in by, and which hath been since walled. This Cathedral doth likewise contain a number of other relics and miraculous pictures to feed the devotion of the vulgar, and bring a constant concourse of people thither.

places were quite unroofed, and only thatched with straw. All the rest appeared in a still more woeful condition, whereever the conquering arms of Lewis XIV. had penetrated, for this was but a few years after the peace of Reswick, so that they had not had time to recover themselves from these dreadful ravages.

An accident happened to me before I had gone far, which, had I been less rash and inconsiderate, might have deterred me from pursuing my sham pilgrimage farther.

It was at the city of Landau, garrisoned by the French, and commanded by an old experienced officer, and was then a very strong place, and the last town they had in Alsace. The familiarity I was observed to carry on with some of the inferior officers and soldiers of the garrison, who were pleased with the whimsical account I gave of myself and my pretended country, made me suspected of being a spy, and as such I was accordingly conducted by a file of musqueteers to the governor, who, not being satisfied with my account, ordered me to be sent to gaol, where I was at first confined in a noisome place for some hours, but afterwards admitted to the liberty of the prison till the next day, when I was conducted in the same manner out of the city, and forbid, under the severest penalties, to return into it[3].

This dreadful escape might, one would think, have opened my eyes to see the folly and danger of my ill-concerted scheme, as well as reminded me of my promise of returning to my poor anxious mother, if I did not think fit to stay with my father. But my religion and prudence were much of a piece, just sufficient to

---

3   In this fabulous account I gave of myself, prefixed to the history of Formosa, I pretended to have been seized here for taking a plan of the fortifications of the place, which was absolutely false, for though I had done so more than once in my native country, where I could give no umbrage, I was not so stupid as to do so in this; neither was it consistent with my scheme to pretend to any skill in drawing and fortifications. However, as to the governor of the place it is most likely that my youth and simplicity moved his pity more than any credit he could give to what I said for myself, for excepting my making a longer stay in it than is usual for pilgrims, there had been nothing said or done by me that could give the jealousy of my being a spy.

make me apply myself to heaven in time of danger, which was no sooner blown over, but I as quickly forgot what I owed to either, except that I looked on myself as obliged to assist at the church offices, such as mass, vespers, &c. as often as opportunity offered, which I continued doing till a more wicked and abominable project made me leave it off. These particulars may perhaps be thought too trifling to my readers to be worthy inserting, but to me they appear in a quite other light, and do but too plainly shew how naturally one miscarriage draws on a worse, where religion and reason have unhappily lost their influence, or yielded it to a predominant and ungovernable passion, and how easily the indulging of it will, by degrees, come to quench all remorse and conviction, and unless the Divine Grace interposes, hurry a man into utter perdition. And as no man hath more sensibly felt the sad effects of the one, as well as the blessed ones of the other, what can I do less than acknowledge and adore that divine and undeserved mercy, to which alone I owe so great, and I hope effectual, deliverance? And what cause have I not to be, to the highest degree, thankful that I had such early impressions of religion inculcated into my mind, and which tho' suppressed and smothered for a long time, by the violence of a favourite vice, did yet, in God's own time, bring me into a sense and abhorrence of my past follies, and, in some measure, drove me from the most dreadful danger into the arms of a merciful and forgiving Saviour, and that in so wonderful and unhoped for a manner, that it was impossible for me to attribute the blessed change to any thing but to a supernatural grace and mercy?

I shall, however, in the sequel, be more succinct, especially in my account of what happened to me from Landau, to the fatal time in which I was unwarily drawn into the most abandoned piece of imposture, that of my pretended conversion to Christianity by Dr. James, then chaplain to a Scotch regiment garrisoned at Sluys; for to mention all those particulars would not only appear a most stupid and tedious, but an almost incredible series of the most unaccountable follies and disasters that any rash youth could fall into. It will be sufficient to say, that I travelled several hundred leagues through Germany, Brabant and Flanders, under the notion of a Japanese converted to Christianity by some jesuit missionaries, and brought to Avignon, by them to be farther instructed, as well as to avoid the dreadful punishment inflicted on all that turn Christians in the dominions of the emperor of Japan. In pursuance of which shameful pretence, I kept up an outward form or religion, was frequent at church, and was sometimes affected with those duties, and, at other times, pinched with a transient remorse and shame at the consciousness of the wicked part I was then acting. My fluency in the Latin tongue, and smattering of other branches of learning, especially logic, philosophy and theology, of which my tenacious memory still preserved some of the most curious parts, joined to the flagrant account I gave of myself, procured me, indeed, more regard and a greater share of beneficence, than was commonly shewed to other travellers or pilgrims, but my carelessness and extravagance not suffering me to lay out any money in dress, or even linnen, to keep me clean and decent, I, by degrees, made so dismal and shabby an appearance, that I outdid the very common beggars, and this misfortune brought on worse upon me. For first, it gave such an ill face and discredit to all my pretences, as all my learning could not counterbalance; and 2dly, when I came into some considerable cities, which I was desirous to see, and where they have hospitals for pilgrims and strangers, with suitable accommodations according to their rank, appearance, or recommendation, commendation, I shewed, in vain, my counterfeit pass, which, if I had been in a better trim, would, from the advantageous manner in which I had dressed it,

have procured a much better reception; those who attend on such
occasions would seldom give themselves the trouble of reading
it, though I begged of them so to do, but, taking it for granted,
that I was one of the lowest rank, or deserving to be treated
as such, did generally herd me among the meanest, by which
I saw myself in a short time covered with rags and vermine,
and infected with a most virulent itch. This dismal plight, one
would have thought sufficient, to rouse me from my senseless
lethargy, and make me follow the example of the returning
prodigal, especially, as I found, to my great mortification, that
all my fair shew of learning, made me appear now only the
more despicable in the eyes of the soberer part; for how could
even those, who gave any credit to what I told them, forbear
supposing that I must have been guilty of some great enormity,
or else the Jesuits, by whom I pretended to have been brought
out of Japan into Avignon, would never have given me up to
so shameful a vagabond life; and no doubt but the far greater
part believed it all a forgery, though they did not think it worth
the while to have me called to an account for it. Thus did I find
my affairs grow from bad to worse, insomuch that I was often
pinched with want, and glad would I have been to have returned
home to my mother; but the thought of my present condition
would not permit me to think of it, and, perhaps, I could have
preferred any death to so great a mortification as it would have
been both to her and me. I have, however, had reason to think it
a mercy that I had such an inveterate itch, added to all my other
misfortunes, for I perceived that in several great cities of Brabant
and Flanders, there are a sort of procuresses, who wander about
the streets under the character of Begines[4], and pick up all the

---

4   The true Begines are a good sort of unmarried women, who dedicate themselves to
    works of charity; but instead of being cloistered up like nuns, visit the houses of the
    poorer sort, and procure them all proper relief from the charitable rich. They likewise
    extend their care to the sick, lame, prisoners and strangers, and are known by a particu-

likely fellows they meet with, in order to make a lewd trade of them; and I being then very young, sanguine, and likely in person, have now and then been invited and led by them in a seeming hospitable manner, to some charitable ladies to receive, as was pretended, some token of their generosity, but, in reality, to return a less commendable one to the benefactress. But my distemper, whether or no it was imagined to be of a worse kind than it was, proved such a disgustful bar, that I never was put to the trial, otherwise I am sure neither my virtue nor prudence would have been proof against it; for though I was then absolutely innocent of any criminal commerce with any of the sex, yet, circumstanced as I was, I have reason to believe I should easily have yielded at any hazard, and this further consideration made me still more weary of my wretchedness.

I was at length come to the celebrated city of Liege, and stayed some time there, to view all the curiosities of the place, and at night took up my lodging at the hospital, where we were likewise allowed some kind of supper. There I was informed that an officer was arrived at one of the suburbs belonging to the Dutch, who inlisted people into the Dutch service, and gave good encouragement to such vagrants as appeared fit to carry a musket. I had no great hopes that I should pass muster with him, being both too young and short, as I thought, for his purpose: however, I resolved to try, and soon persuaded half a dozen of my fellow ragamuffians to follow me; but as nobody could have a greater aversion than I to a soldier's life, by what I had seen at my native place, where was always kept a strong garrison, I began to wish I might meet with a repulse. The rest were presently inlisted by the pretended officer, for he only bought them to sell

---

lar plain dress, not unlike that of the nuns. But there are also many vile women, who, under the cloak of that dress and character, carry on the trade of procuresses, and are but too commonly encouraged and supported in it, by the profligate rich and great.

them again; but when he came to me, and had heard my patched up story, instead of seeming discouraged from taking such a raw and tender boy, he really, to my great surprize, shewed me an uncommon regard, tho' I made the worst figure of any of his recruits; and I could by no means conceive the reason of it till near a month after, during which time we were well entertained at an inn, wanting for neither victuals nor drink. He soon observed me to be averse to strong liquors, and indulged me in it. At length, having sold away all his recruits but me, he began to tell me that he had too great a regard for me, to send me with them to carry a brown musket, and that he designed something better for me, and more suitable to my education; but that he must first try to get me cured of the scabious disease, which by that time had spread itself all over my skin. Accordingly he tried all proper medicines, got me physicked, anointed, blooded, bathed, &c. but without success. Being at length obliged to return to his then home, he got me handsomely equipt, and took me to Aix-la-Chapelle, where I found he kept a grand coffee-house, and billiards, and other games, in the most handsome part of the city, over against the town-hall, and here I was to wait on the customers, and to teach a boy of his to read, &c.

I had reason to believe that my new-master had conceived hopes that I should bring a good number of customers to his house; and, as for myself, I expected to find no small satisfaction in being seen, and suffered to display my parts among them. But we found ourselves both disappointed, in a great measure, because, tho' it was then the heighth of the season for drinking the waters, and the town was full of people; yet the greatest part of them were seldom to be seen any where but at the pump, and the walks about it, and these were at another and distant part of the town; so that there was hardly any resorted to his coffee-house, except gentlemen that came thither to spend an hour or two at billiards, backgammon, basset, or some other game, and these were men of little or no taste for learning, except two or three French refugees, who appeared to me to be professed gamesters. These, and now and then some German gentlemen, that dropped in by chance, would condescend to divert themselves with my company, question me about variety of things, and hold an argument with me about some curious or instructing subject, and at their going away commonly left some marks of their generosity, which, however, my master gave me to understand, I was to be contented with such a share of as he should please to allow me.

Besides his coffee-house, he furnished the balls, and other places of that resort, with lemonade, orgeat, and other cooling liquors proper for the season, as well as with variety of drams for such as liked them. And here it was that I beheld the beau monde in such extraordinary splendor, as was like to have been of the most fatal consequence to me, and to have drove me to the most desperate piece of folly and madness that a man in his senses could have been guilty of, and which I shall forbear mentioning, merely for the ill impression it might be apt to make on some weak and sceptical minds; but which, while I live, I shall never forget, nor cease blessing the divine mercy which kept me back from it. And it was well for me that I was sent thither but once more, tho' another man he kept, much older and fitter for the business, was obliged to give daily attendance there; and I can only think that my cuticular disease, which displayed itself too visibly in my hands, was the cause why I was so seldom sent thither.

Before the season was over, my master, who had other irons in the fire, was obliged to go to Spa, some German leagues from Aix-la-Chapelle, for a fortnight, during which time a great nobleman, at least one who passed for such there, had run himself pretty deep in his debt, by some grand entertainments he had given on several occasions; and it was now whispered about, that he was just on the point of disappearing. My mistress, upon the first hint of it, told me I must immediately set out and fetch her husband. The time was so short, and the way so long and difficult, considering that I was to go on foot, that there was scarcely any probability of my reaching the place time enough, and much less so, considering I was a stranger to the road and to the language, that I would have willingly excused myself from it, and have persuaded her to have dispatched a man and horse to him, but she was a haughty dame, and above being advised, so that I was forced to comply, though without any hopes of getting there time enough, in which case it would be of no service to him, especially if I should chance to lose my way, of which there was so much the more danger, as it was very intricate, and I knew not a step of it, nor how to be informed about it, for want of the German tongue. And indeed, though I took all the care I could, I found before I was got half way to the place, that it would be impossible for me to avoid being so often out, through the various windings and turnings, and cross-roads I frequently met with, that I despaired of reaching it in double the time. The anxiety and fear I was in was so great, about the reception I should meet with, both from him and her for my succeeding so ill, that I began to think of preventing it, by giving them both the slip. My heart, however, hesitated a good while, and upbraided me with the ingratitude and injustice I was going to be guilty of, as likewise with the danger I might incur, should I be caught afterwards by him; for in such a case, I must have expected nothing less than the highest marks of his resentment. But when I considered, on the other hand, that all my care and diligence could not bring me to him time enough, and that I should be ill treated for that which I could not avoid, I preferred a distant danger to one seemingly at hand; and being then just going to cross a high road, which I was told led to the city of Cologn, immediately took to it, with a resolution to return to my father, and then to my mother, by the same way I had formerly gone. This last consideration was then strong with me, as it revived in my mind the concern and grief they must be in about me, especially my poor mother, who had heard nothing from me since that melancholy letter I sent to her upon leaving my father. The thoughts of seeing again two such dear parents, had so enlivened me, that it had in a great measure effaced all other reflections, particularly the remorse of my ingratitude to my late master. But here I was again disappointed, not only of that happiness, but even from the very prospect and hopes of it, and that justly too, and by my own stupid folly. And since the Divine Providence had so wonderfully delivered me from the dangers and miseries of a soldier's life, by inspiring my master with sentiments, whether of gain or pity, or both, and I had made such ungrateful returns, both to God and him, it was but just I should plunge myself into the misery and danger I was so unworthy to escape.

I had already passed through Cologn, and Bon the residence of the elector of Cologn, and got to another city of his electorate likewise on the Rhine, when upon my entering it at one of the gates, I was accosted by a person genteely dressed, who, among several other questions, asked me if I was willing to enter into that elector's service, and used some of the usual topicks to induce me to it. I was surprised at his question, and readily enough answered in the negative, but was soon after persuaded by him to accept his offer, tho' without the least force or circumvention, and merely by my own weakness and stupidity, or rather some judicial fatality, for nothing less than that I should think could have made me alter the laudable resolution I had taken, or so easily set aside the thoughts of revisiting and reviving two such dear and afflicted parents once more, after I was got so far in the way to it; but this was not the only misfortune that attended this rash and unnatural action, which rather proved the fatal source of new scenes of miseries and wickedness.

The liberty that is commonly granted to soldiers to swear, game, drink, whore, &c. is very great among the Germans, and much more among the French; these last may be justly affirmed to be the most profligate of any I ever have known or read of. There is no crime or lewdness they will not commit, no oaths or curses so terrible they will not delight in. They seem destitute of all sense of religion and shamefacedness, and so wholly careless about a future state, that I have seen many of them go to the gallows for desertion with as much unconcern, and some of them with a seeming jocundity, as if they were mounting the guard; and not one of them did I ever observe to shew the least sign or repentance, fear of death, or concern about another life. Those we had in this regiment were, if possible, still worse, being mostly deserters from the French service, and to the last degree profligate: and if there was any one among them that was more soberly or religiously inclined, he was sure to become the object of their scorn and contempt, and to be baited like some wicked or monstrous creature, a vast number of which we had in this regiment; and these, coming to be intermixed with a number of raw young German recruits, taken some from the plough and cart, others from their trades, and some even from the Universities, did debauch them into all manner of wickedness. This was the unhappy herd I was now got among, and whose company and example compleated my ruin, by extinguishing those few faint traces of religion I had left. I was indeed neither inclined to drinking nor gaming, and was not hardened enough in impudence to follow them in their lewdness; but was bad enough, nevertheless, to indulge myself, in order to appear as vile and abandoned as they, in a shameful habit of uttering such new and fashionable oaths, and monstrous curses, as I had lately rather heard with horror, than learned, at Aix-la-Chapelle; and as I was still as ambitious as ever to pass for a Japonese, chose to profess myself an unconverted or heathenish one, rather than what I had then pretended to be, a convert to Christianity. My vanity soon made me begin to make an aukward jest and ridicule of the most solemn and sacred truths of the Gospel, and to take a brutish delight at the surprize which the more sober people of the town I conversed with, expressed at my blasphemous and prophane expressions and objections, as well as in the pleasure I observed this gave to my fellow-soldiers, or rather fellow-brutes.

As the former had observed me to be, in all other respects, a sober young fellow, given to no vice; and found me likewise master of some sense and learning, they began to express an uncommon compassion for me, and, believing me a heathen indeed, proposed to me to enter the lists with some of their learned priests or monks, who, they doubted not, would easily convince me of my error and danger; tho' they themselves had not been able to do it. It can hardly be doubted, but such a vain abandoned fellow as I was, would readily accept the offer. To have declined, would have betrayed a diffidence I was not capable of; so that I pleased myself with having a fair opportunity of displaying my parts and learning against my antagonists, and either to stand proof against all their arguments, or yield myself convinced by them, according as I should find it suit best with my vanity or interest; for if I found it worth my while to chuse the latter, I thought I should appear to the world as a convert of uncommon size, and gain no small applause by it. There was but one thing could make me hesitate about it, viz. the horrid guilt I should plunge myself into by such a vile piece of hypocrisy, and I own it made some impression upon my mind; but it proved short-lived, and my own sanguine temper soon got the mastery of it, and I at length consented to be introduced to a Capuchin of that city, who was esteemed a man of great piety as well as learning, and who had been apprised before of the intended visit, and the purport of it.

When we came to the monastery, we found the good old capuchin sitting on a bench, in an outward room of it, facing the gate, with a lusty young woman kneeling before him, barking like a dog, and making a great many other antick noises and postures; upon which I was told that she was possessed, and that the good father was exorcising the evil spirit out of her. Whether she was then sent for on purpose, or came by accident, I know not; but I remembered to have seen her at some processions, and once or twice at church, in the same unaccountable attitudes; and, as I was then weak enough to think it a real possession, from her extravagant actions and words, I began to fear, so great is the power of guilt on some occasions, that the devil might either expose me for the vile part I was then acting, or perhaps do me some other and worse mischief, as he had formerly done to those vagabond exorcists of whom we read Acts xix. 16. to avoid which I withdrew as soon as I decently could, as if to leave him to go on with his exorcism. Whether he took it in this sense or not, I know not; but at our next meeting, when she was out of the way, he took occasion from thence to prove the truth of the Christian religion in general, and of the church of Rome in particular; and that her priests alone have the power of casting out devils. I told him, with a smile, that it would be time enough to insist on the miracle, or enquire into the reality of it, when it was actually performed; to which he replied, with an air of great pity and seriousness, that God did frequently permit such poor creatures to be tormented for some time, before he vouchsafed them a deliverance; but that tho' exorcisms and prayers would not avail till then, yet they were obliged in charity to make use of them, in hopes that they would one time or other prove successful.

As we came to enter into other arguments, I found that the good old Capuchin was better provided for a controversy against Protestants than against heathens, which gave me no small advantage against him; and this I took with such an assuming air, and lightness of mind, that could not but be displeasing to him; this was so natural to me, that I never could forbear displaying it upon all such occasions, and no wonder if it gave them great cause to think me either not serious enough for the momentousness of the dispute, or perhaps rather that I was nothing less than what I pretended to be. I cannot indeed recollect, that any thing like this last was their real judgment of me, from any thing that dropped from them, though it was but too visible to be the case, if their charity did not blind their judgment in my favour; however, I could see plainly enough from their uneasiness, that they were not likely to be very forward in repeating our conferences, and I was vain enough to impute it to my being an overmatch for them in the dispute. And it was in the same vain boasting strain, that I affirmed in that fabulous account I gave of myself in England, that I was discharged out of that service for being a heathen, and for refusing to yield to the arguments of those who had attempted to convert me. The assumption was absolutely false, and I was discharged by order of the colonel, because I was not only below the standard, but also too tender for the fatigues of a soldier's life. And indeed I cannot express the miseries we underwent in the service of that prince, who was then so eminently poor, that great numbers of his troops perished for want of cloaths, fewel, and even of bread; and had I not been treated with greater care and tenderness than most of the rest were, must inevitably have perished in a very hard winter at Bon, where, besides the want of all other necessaries, the greatest part of the garrison were quartered in barracks open to all winds and weather, and forced to lie on the bare boards.

Being thus happily discharged from so dreadful a slavery, it was natural for me to think once more of returning to my long-wished-for home, at any rate, and at all hazards; but here likewise my ill fate had laid an unexpected obstacle, which it was not in my power to remove; for my late captain, a sordid wretch, who had been raised to his post from that of a common centinel, by the basest means, had taken those cloaths I had brought from Aix-la-Chapelle under his care, and, as he pretended, to prevent my selling them, and spending the money; but upon my being discharged, refused to restore them to me, though he stripped me of my ammunition ones, and had the conscience to send me away in the heart of a severe winter, with a bare loose old frock of blue linnen, and without waistcoat or shoes to my feet, for those he gave me were .o worn out that my feet touched the ground, so that I could never have travelled far before the hardness of the weather would have made an end of me. This made me resolve to go back to Cologn, and try how far my dismal plight and fluent tongue would work upon peoples charity; but it being then wartime, I was stopped, as is usual in garrisoned cities, at the gate, and conducted to the main guard, to give an account of myself to the officer then on duty. I did so, and lighted on a person, who was really a gentleman, and took such liking to me, that I listed myself in his company, and was presently after supplied with cloaths fitter for the season. I passed to him for a Japonese and a heathen, and was entered in his company under the name of Salmanazar, which, since my coming into England, I altered, by the addition of a letter or two, to make it somewhat different from that mentioned in the book of Kings, but whether my new captain believed what I told him or not, I became no small favourite of his. He was a man of good sense, spoke Latin and French well, and had some good scholars in his company, one or two of them of the church of Rome, whereas the regiment consisted mostly of Lutherans, it belonging to the duke of Mecklenburg, but was then in the Dutch pay, and garrisoned at Cologn.

That great city is, perhaps, one of the most superstitious in all Germany; every street and every house hath the statue or image of some saint or other, to which they light candles at night, but mostly to that of the Virgin Mary. Our Lutherans, in spight of all prohibitions from the magistracy, could not forbear shewing their dislike and contempt to these, and many other superstitious customs they beheld, and were sometimes punished for it. Yet did not this deter me from taking pride in outdoing them, though I was so far from having the same laudable pretence for it, that in my heart I condemned them for their untimely zeal, and myself for my impious vanity. We had likewise several loose gentlemen brought up in some of the best universities, who had been prevailed upon to exchange their gowns and books for a musket; some of them were Protestants, others Papists, and with these our chief officers delighted to set me on disputing, by which I had gained their ill will so far, as I generally proved too hard for them, that they had stigmatized me with the titles of heathen, infidel unbaptized, and the like; but these, instead of giving me any uneasiness or remorse, rather soothed my pride, and made me now and then, upon a proper occasion, take delight to remind them that I could give better reasons for my being so, than they could for themselves. My captain thinking that our chaplain, who had been brought up a regular clergyman in the Lutheran way, might succeed better with me, proposed a conference to him; but he being a bashful young gentleman, modestly declined it, and contented himself with exposing the folly and absurdity of the heathenish religion in some of his sermons, where he had a large field to expatiate on, without the danger of opposition. I was afterwards introduced to two others, one who served the Lutheran meeting at Cologn (for they tolerate Protestant meetings in time of war for the use of the garrison, though they shut them up in time of peace) and the other a man of great learning, at a small distance from the city. Our disputes proved but of short duration, I always attacking them upon such points, as I knew they were the least able to defend, but by Scripture, which I pretended not to believe, but urged even those very points, such as the Trinity, Consubstantiation, &c. as arguments against it; and this, as well as my vain and assuming behaviour, might easily raise a dislike, if not more likely, a mistrust of me. One thing I had occasion to observe, that where Papists and Protestants are so intermingled, their guides are better stored with arguments against each other, than against the common enemies of the Christian faith.

From Cologn we were ordered into Holland by the next spring, and began to encamp as soon as the campaign began. The Lutherans and Calvinists had prayers morning and night at the head of every regiment, and a sermon on Sundays, and I was vain enough to go from one to the other to observe their method of devotion, and singing of psalms and hymns, at which they both behaved with great seriousness: but as for me, after listening awhile to them, I was commonly driven by my rashness and vanity to turn my back to them, and turning my face to the rising or setting sun, to make some aukward shew of worship, or praying to it, and was no less pleased to be taken notice of for so doing. This vain fit grew up to such a height, that I made me a little book with figures of the sun, moon and stars, and such other imagery as my phrensy suggested to me, and filled the rest with a kind of gibberish prose and verse, written in my invented character, and which I muttered or chanted as often as the humour took me.

I have often justly wondered at the singular goodness of God to such a vile abandoned wretch as I was become by this time, that in neither regiment, in which I had continued, as I remember, about two years, during which a sharp and severe war was carried on with equal fierceness, it never was my lot to be commanded to a siege, battle, party, skirmish, or place of danger, in which I might have been suddenly cut off in the midst of a most impious career; or, what is equally surprising, that the apprehension of so dreadful an end, should not have deterred me from so senseless and wicked a course, and made me feel the monstrous stupidity of running such desperate hazards of body and soul, for the sake of a little popular admiration at the best; but, instead of which, I have more frequently met with mortification and contempt. But I was still very young, to the best of my remembrance not above eighteen, if quite so much; my mind misguided by a wrong education, as I have before observed; conscious of my own want of any real merit, and yet fond to excess for any kind of pretence to it; and so desirous of being admired and taken notice of, that, rather than have foregone that favourite passion, I would have chosen to indulge it, I verily believe at that time, at the hazard and expence of being looked upon as the very vilest fellow that ever lived. As for those impressions of religion which I had so strongly imbibed in my youth, they gradually lost their influence in proportion to my giving way to that destructive passion, and, at the best, were more in my head than in my heart, till it pleased the divine grace to transplant them thither, as the properest soil for their fructifying; but this blessing did not come down to me till after several years, and a variety of scenes of impiety and guilt. I shall pass by the other occurrences of my soldier's life, to come to that fatal one which proved the source of new and more horrid offences against God and man.

The last garrison I came to was at Sluys, where was a French and a Scotch regiment in the Dutch pay. There I soon became acquainted with several of the French officers, whose language I perfectly understood; but as I was wholly unacquainted with the Scotch and English, and few of them could speak Latin, I could not be so conversant with them. I found most of those French gentlemen very superficial, and did not a little indulge my vanity in ridiculing their tenets, whether they were Papists or Protestants, for there was a mixture of them, and had occasion to observe (tho' to my shame, had I had the least sense of the vile part I played) that, tho' the greater number of them were given to such flagrant vices as are but too common among gentlemen of that profession; yet they all appeared so firmly attached to the tenets of their particular churches, that they expressed much more uneasiness at those sarcasms I used to throw out, than they did at the most dreadful oaths they commonly swore, or any vices that reigned among them. And as I still kept myself untainted from the latter, and had long ago broke myself of that horrid one of swearing, which I had taken up on my first entrance into the soldier's life (not so much indeed out of a principle of religion, as from an ambition I had of passing for a moral heathen) I frequently used to observe to them the unreasonableness of their untimely zeal, which made them so readily condemn me for what they called my irreligious sarcasms, which yet were but agreeable to my notions and belief, whilst they indulged themselves in vices, such as duelling, wenching, swearing, and drinking, which were not only incompatible with theirs, but such as, bad as they thought me, I could not on any consideration be guilty of. These kinds of severe rebukes ought, I say, to have filled me with the deepest sense of my own more vile and abominable inconsistency; but as that did not so openly appear, the applauses I received from the sober part, and even from some of the ministers, for so strenuously pleading the cause of virtue, made me quite blind to my more odious vices; so that as long as the character or shadow of moral virtue procured me so much regard and esteem, I never troubled myself about the want of the real substance.

Brigadier Lauder, a Scottish gentleman, well respected, and colonel of a regiment in that garrison, was then governor, and, unhappily for me, conceived a curiosity of seeing me at his own house, where were assembled several officers, besides the minister of the French church, and Mr. Innes, chaplain to the Scottish regiment; and after dinner I was admitted to have a kind of conference with them. I own, indeed, that the account I gave of it in that published romance of mine, was far enough from candid or impartial, with respect to the French minister, who was the chief manager in the dispute, my usual vanity having made me relate it too much to his disadvantage, and Mr. Innes, between whom and that gentleman there was a great misunderstanding, added some other particulars, equally misrepresented and mortifying; but, abating that, the rest is the truest part I can call to mind in that forged narrative of myself. However, Mr. Innes, since dubbed doctor by one of the Scotch Universities, and a near relation to the governor, would not lose so fair an opportunity of triumphing over his rival, and finding that I had nonplussed him at almost every argument, but more particularly against that of absolute predestination, took occasion to inform me that it was a doctrine as much condemned by some, as it was strenuously asserted by other churches, and that consequently Christianity, he would undertake to prove, was not to be charged with it. He had a much smoother and less overbearing way of speaking than the other gentleman, and kindly invited me to his lodgings, where we might, at our leisure, discuss that or any other points in dispute, not doubting but a person of my sense, learning, and seeming candor (as he was pleased to compliment my vanity) would easily yield to conviction, when the point was once cleared to my satisfaction, as he did not doubt he should shortly do.

I readily accepted of his invitation, by which I found he designed to exclude the French minister from having any share in our future conferences, but did not then suspect his farther drift, which was, if he could, at any rate, or by any means, make a convert of me, to recommend himself to the then worthy bishop of London, a person, he knew, of such singular candor, as not to be over suspicious, and too generous not to encourage what he thought a charitable, worthy action; so that, as I easily found afterwards, the hopes of procuring some preferment to himself, rather than any regard or concern for me, was the main spring of all his pretended zeal for my conversion. I am sorry that I shall be obliged, in the sequel, to relate several very harsh truths concerning his behaviour on this scandalous occasion, though I will be still careful to mention no more of it than is barely necessary to set the matter in a true light, and rather conceal than expose such parts of it, as have not an immediate relation to the subject I am upon; much less will I go about to aggravate his faults, in order to extenuate my own. If he should be still alive when these memoirs shall be published, will not be the first thing that has been published with truth and justice to his disadvantage, and may all contribute to inspire him with a true remorse and sincere repentance: if dead, it can neither hurt him, nor any that belong to him[5].

---

5   The doctor is long since dead, and, I am sorry to say, hath left a character behind him that reflects no great credit to how's cloth, and may easily, among those that knew him, justify what I have already said, and shall be farther obliged to mention in the sequel, he was not many years older than I when I first came acquainted with him, and I soon perceived to be a man of no small ambition, though he was so far from having any of the generous disposition which is mostly known to accompany it, that he was no less a slave to avarice: witness his abrogating to himself the credit as well as advantage of that excellent treatise,

He was, however, intent upon his pursuit, and so assiduous in sending for me, that some of the Dutch ministers thought fit likewise to do the same, and more particularly, as I found afterwards, to reconcile me to their favourite article of predestination, by expounding it to me according to what they call the infralapsarian system, which is indeed less dreadful and antiscriptural; but Mr. Innes easily dissuaded me from going amongst them, that he might have me wholly to himself, and seldom failed at our parting to clap a small piece of Dutch silver into my hand, which proved an effectual bait to me, who was still so bad an oeconomist of my poor soldier's pay, and then wanted several necessaries, with which this supplied me.

By this time I began not to be a little tired with a soldier's life, the place was very cold and bleak, the duty hard, and the pay so small, that even they who could make the most of it, could but just make shift to live on the plainest things; so that all things considered, there was no likelihood I should make any long opposition to his arguments, especially as he took care to back them with very large promises of getting my discharge, and bringing me into England, where he made me hope to meet with the greatest encouragement, and I own that the prospect of such a change of life made so great an impression upon me, that he rather found me more forward to answer his design than was consistent with prudence, and too ready to be wholly directed by him. As soon as I had given him this assurance, he wrote a long

---

intituled, A Modest Enquiry after Moral Virtue, for which he obtained from the present bishop of London a very good living in Essex; but which the real and worthy author, a poor episcopal clergyman in Scotland, since obliged him publicly to disown and disclaim in print, as well as to compromise with him for the profit of the edition. This, together with his malversation in sundry respects in the parish of St. Margaret, Westminster, still fresh in people's memory, obliged him to retire to his new living, where, I am told, he lived very private, and, I hope, made the best use of his solitude. As therefore he had long ago lost his character among all that knew him, or had heard of his shameful actions, I thought myself less obliged to treat it with that tenderness that I should have done, had he taken more care to conceal his vile actions from the world.

letter to the bishop of London, wherein he told me he had said so
many things in my favour, that he doubted not of my soon being
sent for by, and meeting with the kindest reception from him.
However, the wished-for answer not coming till six or seven
weeks afterwards, gave me an opportunity of seeing farther into
his temper, than I had been able to do; his messages to me were
gradually less frequent, our interviews more cold, as well as our
parting, when he likewise with-held his hand from making me
the usual presents. This latter I indeed supposed might be owing
to his cash running lower than usual; but I have seen so many
instances of his nigardness, that I have more reason to impute it
to that, and partly to his despairing of the success of his letter; for
whilst he was in hopes of it, he had taken care to introduce me
to some learned gentlemen, ministers and others, under pretence
of examining whether I was capable of giving a satisfactory
account of my pretended conversion, and had obtained from
some of them very advantageous certificates in my favour, which
he took no small pride to shew to the brigadier and to his other
acquaintance; but upon the unexpected delay of the answer,
he behaved with more coldness and indifference, till a jealous
thought started in his mind, lest that should encourage some of
these ministers, who had expressed themselves in my favour, to
take the business out of his hand, and rob him of the credit of
his new convert. This suspicion made him all at once alter his
behaviour, and resolve to baptize me with such haste and so little
warning, that my surprize gave me no time to consider what an
abominable piece of irreligion I had engaged myself in, though
I must confess, to my shame; that had he given me more time to
think upon it, yet I have but too much reason to think, his fair
promises and delusive prospects would easily have swallowed
up all my scruples and reluctance, upon his first renewal of them.

This, and some other parts of his behaviour, had already

convinced me that a charitable design of converting a soul was the farthest from his thoughts, and that he was so far from believing me to be what I pretended, that he had some time before taken a most effectual way to convince himself of the contrary, beyond all possibility of doubting. His stratagem, if I may so call it, was to make me translate a passage in Cicero de natura deorum, of some length, into my (pretended) Formosan language, and give it to him in writing; and this I easily did, by means of that unhappy readiness I had at inventing of characters, languages, &c. But, after he had made me construe it, and desired me to write another version of it on another paper, his proposal, and the manner of his exacting it, threw me into such visible confusion, having had so little time to excogitate the first, and less to commit it to memory, that there were not above one half of the words in the second that were in the first. His desiring me to construe this likewise, confused me still more; especially, when he shewed me the palpable difference. The serious air he assumed upon it, made me expect nothing else than a total rupture, and his exposing the imposture in the manner I was conscious it deserved. I was however agreeably (and, to my shame, I ought to add) deceived; and he finding, by this unexpected trial, what a memory and readiness I had, and how qualified I was to carry on such a cheat, began to clear his brow, and calm the disorder he had thrown me into, by a more chearful and friendly look; but did not forget, at the same time, to give me to understand, tho' at a great distance, that I ought to take care to be better provided for the future. I promised to take his advice, and did so in part; but was become too indolent to go thro' the fatigue of forming a whole language, at least till I was convinced that it would stand me in some stead; though, by what I have tried since I came into England, I cannot say but I could have compassed it with less difficulty than can be conceived, had I been capable of applying closely to it. However, his continuing his assiduity and seeming regard for me, at least till the delay of the bishop's answer, which made him suspend it for ten or twelve days, gave me but too much reason to think, that he had not one jot more of conscience or religion than I, tho' older, and a learned divine, since he made no scruple not only to join in, but to encourage and pursue so vile a cheat. But if he had no more religion, he had at least more worldly prudence than I, in that he laid the foundation for some considerable preferment for himself; whilst I, like the stupid abandondoned wretch I had been hitherto, looked no farther than a little vain satisfaction for the present, or, at most, a deliverance from the soldier's life. For by that time I could see so far thro' all his artifices, and different behaviours, that I did not much depend on any of his other promises. And he soon after gave me cause to think myself not mistaken in him. For when, upon his bringing me into England, he got himself into the post of chaplain-general of the English forces in Portugal, by the interest of the good bishop Compton, he not only left me to shift for myself, and to bear the brunt of all objections, but was guilty of such other vile actions, as easily convinced me that he was a more real convert to Spinozism, than I was to him; for I observed him often reading that author's posthumous works, tho' he was an utter stranger to his sober way of living. I had likewise a greater opinion of his parts and learning, than I have since found cause for, which made me conclude, that I had no reason to be more scrupulous than he, and this in a great measure quelled all my slight and transitory qualms, at least till it came to the solemn push.

I have already hinted, that his fear of being supplanted by some other minister, made him resolve to hasten the impious ceremony, for so I thought it, whatever he did; but of this he had apprised me only in general terms, and without fixing any time for it, or mentioning how he designed to perform it, probably

that I might think the less upon it. Accordingly some days passed
without my seeing him, or at least hearing any thing about it,
when one afternoon he sent his man to my lodgings, to acquaint
me that he had fixed that evening about six of the clock for it, and
to desire me to be ready against the time. As I had hardly three
hours to consider of it, one may easily imagine the surprise and
hurry, the confusion and dread, it threw me into; and, indeed, I
was so divided between the fear of bringing upon myself some
heavy judgment for so impious a prophanation of that divine
institution, and the thoughts, if I submitted to it, of behaving
with some proper decency under all those tumults with which
my mind was then agitated, that I began to wish I might have
resolution enough to avoid it, when the dreaded time was come.
But that not only failed me, when I saw the governor and several
other officers and gentlemen going to the chapel, where the mock
ceremony was to be dispatched; but the devil, I believe, did then
find a way of calming my conscience for the present, by putting
it into my head that it being to be performed by a heretic, for such
I then judged, if not all the Protestant ministers, at least such a
one as I now knew my ungodly guide to be, it could be indeed
no sacrament, nor a repetition of it. And this confused distinction
I then called to mind from what I had learned at the schools,
tho' I was far enough from being satisfied that it was right. What
salvo he had for himself, I can only guess; but, as far as I could
perceive, he went thro' the ceremony with a very composed
countenance and presence of mind, and seeming devotion; and
tho' he only had his English common-prayer book before him,
yet he read the office all in a good Latin off-hand, as the saying is,
and without any hesitation or solecism, as those observed who
heard him with greater attention than I was then capable of. For
tho' I was a perfect master of the Latin, and he pronounced it,
as most of his countrymen do, in a very intelligible manner; yet

such was my confusion and hurry of spirits, that I scarcely knew or could mind one word he said. And a much greater one, I dare affirm, I should have been in, had I been either able to attend to the solemnity of the office, or had been made acquainted with it before. But I was an utter stranger to every part of it; and it is my opinion, that he chose I should be so, for he never once shewed, much less explained, the least part of it in any of the meetings I gave him at his lodgings. All I could recollect of the whole, was that I kept up so much presence of mind, as to appear demure and serious all the while, which I thought very long, and that I was very glad when it was over, and much more so that my abominable hypocrisy had not been detected, or rather punished, by some severe judgment.

The name he gave me was that of George Lauder, which was that of the governor, whom he had prevailed upon to pass for my godfather; and it was accordingly entered into the muster-roll, instead of that of Salmanazar, which I had till then answered to. This new name and surname, joined to some congratulations then given me, and a present of a pistole from the governor, made me, for some time, forget the heavy guilt I had plunged myself into. But this calm proved but short, and the delay of the bishop's answer, and much more Mr. Innes's coldness and indifference, after he had once made sure of me, soon brought me to repent of my wicked compliance, as I then judged it, though not so much from a sense of religion, as because I did not look upon my vanity and ambition sufficiently recompensed for the atrocious guilt I had contracted; and this the reader will the better judge by what follows.

The long expected letter came at length; it was full of commendations to Mr. Innes for his zeal, besides a very kind invitation to me from that worthy prelate, to come over into England. I was by that time so weary of a soldier's life, that I should have readily come upon a less promising prospect than that which he now began again to feed my sanguine hopes with. Some things he talked to me quite inconsistent with what, as I before hinted, he knew of me, and which of course could be no temptations to me, unless I was base enough to add still more weight to my guilt; of this kind in particular was what he mentioned to me of a design of sending me to Oxford, to teach the Formosan language to a set of gentlemen, who were afterwards to go with me to convert those people to Christianity, which, if he believed any thing of, he must needs depend upon my inventing such a language, and involving myself in still deeper guilt; and yet I own, to my shame, though I knew not with what view he could mention such a proposal, nor looked upon it but with dread, yet I could not forbear being much elevated with it, though I was still in hopes that I might find some pretence for setting it aside, and being made useful there in some other and more suitable way. How I might have behaved in such a case I know not, only I have reason to question whether I should have had integrity and resolution to have confessed the truth, rather than to have involved myself in a still more shameful imposture; but, as I observed before, I knew him too well to rely on any of his fluent and disingenuous promises.

The governor, at his request, got me discharged, or rather gave my captain another man in my room, whilst Mr. Innes took care to procure a certificate signed by that gentleman and a number of other officers of the garrison, and even by several ministers, much more in my commendation than I could possibly deserve; after which, having got all things in order for our departure, we set out for Rotterdam, where he introduced me to some persons of consideration for piety and learning, particularly the celebrated Mr. Basnage, author of the Continuation of the Jewish History, and likewise to some of the ministers and gentlemen of the English church, and to some of the French Protestants there; among whom I was so much caressed, that I begun to look upon myself in a very agreeable and advantageous light. There were, however, two things that mortified me not a little, viz. the mean appearance I made in some castoff cloaths, with which Mr. Innes had supplied me upon my leaving off my regimental ones, but which were both too big and too long for me, and the shrewd questions put to me by several gentlemen, which convinced me that they did not give all the credit I could have wished, to the account I gave of myself and country. For as to any real remorse or concern for the shameful part I was acting, I found it sit lighter on my mind, in proportion to the many things I met with that flattered my vanity. The more effectually therefore to remove these two obstacles to it, I fell upon one of the most whimsical expedients that could come into a crazed brain, viz. that of living upon raw flesh, roots and herbs; and it is surprising how soon I habituated myself to this new, and, till now, strange food, without receiving the least prejudice in my health; but I was blessed with a good constitution, and I took care to use a good deal of pepper, or other spices, for a concocter, whilst my vanity, and the people's surprize at my diet, served me for a relishing sauce.

We embarked at the Brill for England in the packet-boat, and in our passage had such a dreadful storm, that as many passengers, and among them Mr. Innes, got into the long boat, as it could well contain. They all shewed an uncommon dread in their looks, whilst I, who staid behind, beheld them with a kind of stupid unconcern, rather than a generous pity, every moment in danger of meeting with that dreadful end they had endeavoured to avoid; yet, terrible as the sight was, it hardly raised in me one serious resolution against the more dangerous design I was unhappily embarked in, or the more

dreadful shipwreck I had exposed myself to, that of the soul; or
if any such thoughts came then into my mind, they were soon
dispelled at our landing at Harwich, and at the pleasing prospect
with which Mr. Innes had flattered my ambition and vanity. At
my arrival at London, Mr. Innes, and some worthy clergymen
of his acquaintance, introduced me to the bishop of London, by
whom I was received with great humanity, and got soon after a
good number of friends among the clergy and laity, most of them
persons of piety and worth. But I had a much greater number
of opposers to combat with, who put me under a necessity of
having my senses and memory about me more than ever, to avoid
a fatal detection; for I had been so negligent, notwithstanding
Mr. Innes's caution of being prepared, against exigencies, with
a language and a prudent readiness at reading and writing my
new invented character, that had I been attacked on that side, I
must have been infallibly foiled; but they took a contrary way,
and though they judged rightly of me in the main, yet I can safely
affirm, that they have been very far from being candid, or even
just in the account of the discoveries they pretended to have
made, to my disadvantage; particularly Drs. Halley, Mead and
Woodward; and as I had then several zealous patrons of great
candor and integrity, who made it their business to search into
the bottom of those reports, they found so much sophistry and
disingenuity in them, that I cannot but observe here, that the too
visible eagerness of these gentlemen to expose me, at any rate,
for a cheat, served only to make the more serious and candid part
think the better of me, and to look upon me as a kind of confessor,
especially as the three gentlemen abovementioned, but more
particularly the first, were known to be no great admirers of the
Christian revelation, to which my patrons thought I had given
so ample a testimony. My complexion, indeed, which was very
fair, appeared an unanswerable objection against me; there being

but few such to be met with in those hot climates, especially that of Formosa, which lies under the tropic; but by the help of what I had read or heard of some of those countries, I soon hatched a lucky distinction between those whose business exposes them to the heat of the sun, and those who keep altogether at home, in cool shades, or apartments under ground, and scarce ever feel the least degree of the reigning heat. And this distinction indeed is not only very reasonable, but was afterwards confirmed by persons of candor and experience, who had been in those countries, and affirmed that they had seen persons as fair as any northern Europeans, tho' not in so great a number, that lived under the rays of a vertical sun.

On the other hand, my opposers were as much at a loss how to find out my real country, either by my idiom, or my pronunciation of the Latin, French, Italian, or any other language I was master of. For though this may appear an easy thing to be done, by those who are acquainted with the European languages, and the different pronunciations peculiar to every nation, yet both my idiom and pronunciation were so mixed and blended, and I may say designedly so, by the many languages I had learned, and nations I had been conversant with, that it was impossible for the most curious judge to discover in it any thing like an uniform likeness to any other European one they knew of. Dr. Mead, indeed, took upon him to be very positive from both, that I was of either German or Dutch extract; he could not have pitched upon a more unlikely one, seeing the Dutch idiom and language were the only one I was the least acquainted with, and accordingly some of my friends, who were better judges of such matters, and could plainly see that mine was more opposite to them than to any other, did freely censure him for it, and tell him he might as well have affirmed me to be an Ethiopian from my complexion, as a German from my pronunciation. But the truth

was, I knew enough of all of them to blend my discourse more
or less with any of them, as either to put people upon the wrong
scent, whilst I kept every one from getting into the right one; for
I can safely say that I never met with, nor heard of any one, that
ever guessed right, or any thing near it, with respect to my native
country.

I might here add several visible advantages which my friends
might justly take in my defence, and among them a great number
of scandalous falshoods dispersed abroad from what quarter
I know not, of which those, who were better acquainted with
me, knew me to be wholly innocent, as well as crimes. I was
naturally averse to, such as drinking, gaming, &c. for, bating my
vain-glorious foible, which, though I could not overcome, I took
such care to conceal from them by the most opposite behaviour,
my conversation was such as the most censorious could not
have blamed, but which my friends highly admired in me. The
plainness of my dress and diet, the little trouble I gave myself
about worldly wealth, preferment, or even acquiring or securing
a bare competency, a good-natured and charitable disposition,
visibly natural to me, my averseness to drinking, lewd women,
&c. and a great reservedness to such of the fair sex as had
either lost their reputation, though they lived still in credit and
splendor, and even to those who betrayed too small a regard for
their character, the conversation of whom I professedly avoided,
though against my own interest, not indeed so much from a
principle of virtue, as an affectation of it; these, together with the
warmth I naturally expressed for religion, and the real delight I
took in the public offices of it, appeared such convincing proofs
of my sincerity, that those of my friends, to whom I was most
intimately known, were the most impatient, and displeased
to have it called in question; for who could imagine, as they
often urged, that a youth of so much sense and learning for his

years, so seemingly free from ambition and other vices, could be abandoned enough to be guilty of such abominable an imposture and impiety, for the sake of a little plain, homely food and rayment, beyond which he neither makes the least effort, or seems to have the least wish.

I am aware that what I have said in the last paragraph, will so far carry the face of my once favourite vanity, that it will be censured by several of my readers as a rank piece of ostentation, rather than a sincere acknowledgment of my guilt; tho' a more candid one, who joins both parts of it together, will rather see, that the display of the one, is only the greater aggravation of the other. But as neither was the motive of what I have there said, but rather to do justice to those friends of mine who so kindly took my part on that account, I had much rather undergo censure against myself, than to have omitted any thing that can vindicate their character, and convince the world that the zeal they expressed for me, was really the effect of a most candid and charitable construction on a life so seemingly innocent and disinterested, and not owing to any rash or blind prepossession, or to an unreasonable opposition against my censurers, much less to dishonest connivance with any views or designs of mine; when I am very sure, that if they had had any well-grounded suspicion of my being what I was, an impostor, they would have been the first who would not only have exposed me to the world, but would have become my most irreconcileable enemies. And I thought myself the more obliged, in justice as well as gratitude, to say thus much in their vindication; because some of them, men of probity and learning, undertook to be my advocates in print, and not only complained of those aspersions so freely and unjustly cast upon me, but even challenged my accusers, in several advertisements published in the London Gazzette, to prove any of them against me, or to produce any one solid proof or objection against the account I had given of myself. Notwithstanding, which charitable efforts on my behalf, and the candid vindication they printed some months after, both they and I had the mortification to find (and I have had since great reason to bless God for it) that my fabulous account was as much discredited by the greatest part of the world as ever; which proved an effectual means, in time, to bring me, thro' his mercy, to a deeper sense of my folly and impiety, than I could have been, if that had gained a more general credit.

There was likewise a variety of judgments formed about me, by those who thought me a cheat. Those of the church of Rome believed I was bribed to that imposture by some English ministers, on purpose to expose their church. The Protestants in Holland were much of the same mind; but added, that I was farther hired to explode their doctrine of predestination, and cry up the episcopacy of the church of England, in derogation of their Presbyterian government. Here some represented me as a jesuit or priest in disguise, others as a tool of the nonjurors, because Mr. Innes had introduced me among a set of them, particularly the famed Mr. Lesley, of whose writings, as well as instructive and facetious company, I was very fond; and I may add, that their conversation had not a little biassed me to their principles, especially as I found them so conformable to the school divinity I had learned beyond sea, tho' it never affected me so far as to go to any of their meetings. However, the reader may see, by what I have said hitherto, that all these various opinions were but random shots, and without any foundation. And indeed my case was so intricate and perplexing, that it was next to impossible for the ablest heads to have guessed what my motives were, or for what, or by whom, I was induced thus to impose upon mankind. And I am fully persuaded, that my being wholly innocent of any such vile designs, either against the church or state, or of being employed by the enemies of either, was the cause of my disappointment turning so much to my advantage, which might otherwise have been attended with a more fatal and shameful catastrophe; and that the merciful judge of all hearts, knowing mine to be actuated only by mere youthful folly and vanity, without any other dangerous or guilty design, than the indulging a wild and phrantic passion (which was grown too powerful for me to resist, with that little share of reason and experience I was then master of, and with these disadvantages and temptations I laboured under) did, in his great pity, prevent my going on and perishing under such a load of unrepented guilt, and I accordingly desire to be ever thankful for that great and undeserved instance of his divine mercy and goodness. And, next to my humble acknowledgment of it, I do think myself bound to declare thus solemnly, that I never was set upon, nor directly or indirectly inticed, by any set of men for any private ends, to act the part I did, except what I have lately related of Mr. Innes's encouragements and promises to me, in which I am very well satisfied he had no other ends to serve, but that of his own private interest and advancement.

I am far enough however from reflecting upon, or bearing any resentment against those who looked upon me as a tool of some designing set of men, engaged in some private design. It was not natural to suppose that such a young, and, in all appearance, as well as reality, raw and unexperienced fellow, could of his own head have imbarked in such an imposture, and carried it on so long, and with such boldness and success, as to have procured to himself so many zealous patrons among men of character for learning and probity, unless he had been privately set upon, instructed, and supported in it, by some designing persons of more years, discretion, and abilities, tho' from what quarter was not easy to guess, either from my behaviour, writings, or any view they could perceive me in pursuit of. As for those who took me for a jesuit, priest, or emissary from Rome, they were certainly the widest from the mark. The gentlemen of that church were always my most strenuous opposers, and not without cause, as they could be very sure that whatever design or errand I might be embarked in, it could not be in favour of it; and had my fabulous account met with that credit which it must be supposed was expected, it must have done their cause more disservice than any private design I might carry on could have done good. Besides, it was visible I shunned their company as much as possible, tho' my motive for it, the consciousness of my own guilt, was not so apparent. I never conversed with any of them, but in the jarring and controversial way; and, tho' at that time much against my conscience, was a strenuous opposer of their particular doctrines, both in conversation and writing. I never once entered into any of their chapels, (nor have since, all the time I have been in England) neither did I shew the least favour or partiality towards them. This was indeed rather looked upon as an artifice, said to be very usual and common amongst them, it being urged as an observation of a long standing, that those disguised emissaries affected to appear the most outrageous enemies of that cause they were privately carrying on. Whether the fact be true or not, I can only say, that I never knew of any such but by hearsay; neither am I any farther concerned about it, than to say, that I was the farthest from being one of that sort, and that whatever I have said or written against that church, was only with a view of gaining credit to myself, without any view of serving or hurting it, or indeed caring which of the two was likely to be the result. For tho' all the arguments I had heard or read against it, and in which I was not a little versed, had not yet been able to wipe off the prejudices of my education, which I had imbibed under the jesuits and dominicans, of its being, if not the only saving church as they affirm it to be, yet, at least, of its not being so bad and corrupt, so dangerous and damnable a one as some Protestants, with more zeal than charity, have represented it, under the odious titles of Anti-christ, whore of Babylon, &c. nevertheless, my youth and inconsiderate vanity would not suffer me to enquire whether or no, or how far, I incurred a guilt in my opposing and exposing it.

It was likewise from the same shameful motive of vanity that I pretended, from my own knowledge, not only to confirm but aggravate the black account which authors had published against the jesuits and other missionaries, especially with regard to their boasted conversions and success in the East-Indies, and more particularly concerning the cause of the persecution raised against the Christians in Japan; when all that I knew of it was only from reading or hear-say. And as to the Jesuits, though I was then and am still sensible that some of their maxims, tenets, and politics, do justly deserve to be condemned; yet I was far enough from having such disadvantageous notions of that society, as the world seems generally to have of it, and much less from any thing I had ever observed among them, considering how young I was when I left them, and how close and recluse they keep themselves from the rest of the world. But whether they deserve the disadvantageous character they have, or not, which is best known to him, to whom both they and every man is to give an account at the last great day, it is incumbent upon me thus far to do them justice, as to own, that those reflexions I have cast upon their missionaries in China and Japan, had no other foundation than common report, without any enquiry whether that was true or false; so far was I from having any just or real reason for confirming or aggravating it. As for the rest of the priests of that church, as far as I was capable of judging of them, in those juvenile days in which I was more intimately conversant with several of them, I can only say, with the common voice, that there are good and bad among them, though perhaps to a much higher degree than I have had occasion to observe of those of any other church. One thing I can truly say, however, to their praise, that they generally take greater care to instruct their youth in matters of religion, and to oblige them all to assist at their catechetical lectures on Sundays in the afternoon. The misfortune was, that we had no books to learn them by heart beforehand, but the priest was forced by repetitions to inculcate them in our memories; whence it followed, that those who were wanting either in attention or memory, went away little the better for the pains he took with them. As for me, I never failed coming, because my memory being very tenacious, and my apprehensions pretty quick, I could carry an answer of any length at once or twice repeating, so that I was mostly the first interrogated, and received no small commendations from our instructors, especially as I was one of the youngest, and was as ready at those answers on the next meeting, as if I had thought on nothing else all that time. And as this used to make me to be much admired by the numerous audience, so it of course failed not to feed me with secret pride, and a natural fondness for all such occasions of shewing my talents.

The same happened to me on my coming first into England, when Dr. Innes, proud of his pretended proselyte, introduced me into the company of all the learned divines of his acquaintance, that they might hear me descant on the grounds of my conversion; and I was by that time so well versed in that kind of learning, more from the books I occasionally read on that subject, than from any pains he had taken to instruct me, that I believe few people of my years, notwithstanding I had murdered so much of my time, could have said more in defence of the Christian religion; all which was sufficiently acknowledged with no small commendations and congratulations, both by all that heard me, and by those who have first read these arguments in the fictitious book abovementioned; for that system of religion, and defence of Christianity, was what I had mostly extracted out of Limborch, and some other divines, without Dr. Innes's help, or even knowledge, though what follows there, with respect to Church government, was wholly his, as may be easily perceived from the difference of style and method. However, when all these kinds of conversations were ended, my doctor failed not to spur my pride still farther on, by telling me what those gentlemen said in my commendation, which, whether or not exaggerated by him, gave me such an extraordinary notion of my parts, that I was proud of every opportunity of shewing myself in all companies and public places, without any other view than that of feeding my natural vanity, whilst he was privately pursuing what appeared to him more weighty, the advancing of his fortune, to which end he strove to introduce me, and himself by my means, to all the great men in church and state, which he found no hard matter to do, because, ere I had been in London three months, I had been so cried up for a prodigy, that they were all exceedingly desirous of seeing and conversing with me; and not only the domestic, but even the foreign papers, had helped to blaze forth many things in my praise, for which there was not any foundation. Thus I remember a remarkable article from London, printed in the Dutch and French papers, that the young Japaner had been presented to the archbishop of Canterbury, who admired him chiefly for his readiness in speaking a great variety of languages. Whereas I cannot call to mind that I spoke any but the Latin, which his grace having either forgot, or being unused to my foreign pronunciation, was forced to have interpreted to him, by Dr. Innes, in English. So that I found I needed not to be very solicitous to blow my own trumpet, when the common cry, and the public papers, did it beyond my expectation for me. I had indeed a fluency of the Latin, and a smattering of several modern languages, as well as a great readiness in learning them, had I applied myself to them; but I boasted of more knowledge in them by far than I had, especially in the oriental ones; tho' at that time quite ignorant of them.

I had not been two months in London before the doctor persuaded me to translate the church catechism into my pretended Formosan language; and I, tho' much against my will, was forced, by his overbearing command, not only to perform the odious task, but to present it afterwards to the bishop of London, who received and rewarded it with his usual candor and generosity, and laid it up among his other curious manuscripts, tho' it rather deserved to have been condemned to the flames. However, the doctor had his own views to serve, one of which was to confirm me in the good opinion of that worthy prelate, and of as many other gentlemen as should either see or hear of it. And another, to make me exert my talents in inventing and familiarising myself to this pretended Formosan language and character, for fear my want of it should cause some unexpected discovery, at least before he had got the preferment he was in pursuit of. When I had finished the pretended version, he not only examined it himself carefully, but got other persons to do the same, who all found the language so regular and grammatical, as well as different from all others they knew, both with respect to the words and idiom, that they gave it as their opinion, that it must be a real language, and could be no counterfeit, much less have been invented by such a stripling as I; and hence some of those of my opposers, who thought me a Romish priest in disguise, imagined that I had been assisted in, or taught it, by some of the fraternity beyond sea. I should have observed, that I had taken care to write it in one column in Roman character, with an interlineal Latin version in Italick, and in my invented character on the opposite column.

As he found me to succeed so well in this vile piece of invention, he soon after prevailed upon me to write the history of Formosa, and got several of his and my acquaintance to back the motion, as a thing which would bring much credit and profit to me, and be very acceptable to the public. One might have imagined, that a task so arduous and dangerous would have startled such a raw young fellow as I was, being then scarce twenty years old, and so very great a stranger to these countries. I had indeed got some imperfect notions from a few books that had fallen in my way, as well as from conversation with those who had either been in those parts, or had read more about them than I, but was forced to hatch many things out of my own fertile fancy, to supply the defects of my knowledge. One thing I found a great help and relief from, that the accounts we then had of that island from Candidus, a Dutch minister, who had resided there, and from the rest of the writers who had in some measure copied him, were stuffed with such monstrous absurdities and contradictions, and that the place upon the whole was so very unknown to the Europeans, even to those who had been in China, Japan, and other parts of that country, that I might the more easily make whatever I should say of it, to pass current with the generality of the world. So that without much hesitation I undertook the work, and resolved with myself to give such a description of it as should be wholly new and surprizing, and should in most particulars clash with all the accounts other writers had given of it; particularly that it belonged to Japan, contrary to what all other writers and travellers have affirmed of its being subject to China. And this I was left to hammer out of my own brain, without any other assistance than that of Varenius's description of Japan, which Dr. Innes put into my hands, to get what I could

out of it. All this while both he and the booksellers were so
earnest for my dispatching it out of hand, whilst the town was
hot in expectation of it, that I was scarcely allowed two months
to write the whole, notwithstanding the many avocations I had
by frequent visitors, and invitations abroad. So that it is no
wonder the thing came out so crude, imperfect, and absurd, and
more so would it have been, had not the person, who englished
it from my Latin, assisted me to correct many more and greater
improbabilities, which I had not had time to discover: but he
likewise was hurried on by the booksellers, and had the fewer
opportunities of consulting me on that head. Besides, there was
one maxim I could never be prevailed upon to depart from, viz.
that whatever I had once affirmed in conversation, tho' to ever so
few people, and tho' ever so improbable, or even absurd, should
never be amended or contradicted in the narrative. Thus having
once, inadvertently in conversation, made the yearly number of
sacrificed infants to amount eighteen thousand, I could never be
persuaded to lessen it, though I had been often made sensible
of the impossibility of so small an island losing so many males
every year, without becoming at length quite depopulated,
supposing the inhabitants to have been so stupid as to comply
with, or the priests inhuman enough to have exacted such a
number of human victims. I must moreover observe here, that
my friends found still a much weightier objection against my
account, viz. how such a stripling as I must be when I left that
country (for being then but near twenty years of age I could not
be supposed to have been above fifteen or sixteen, upon my
pretended coming away) could give such a large and particular
account of it, as could hardly have been expected from a man
of twice my age. Many of them were hence inclined to impute
what was so liable to objection in my narrative to my want of
years and experience, which might make me the more liable to

mistake. This, though a very candid excuse for me, I was not inclined to admit of, and therefore, to abate the wonder, was forced, by Dr. Innes's advice, to assume three years more than I had, and to pretend I was nineteen years when I came away, and between twenty-two and twenty-three at the writing of the book; more than that had I pretended to be, my face, air, and behaviour would have given me the lye, for in that only respect did I appear what I really was, a raw, young, hot-headed and inconsiderate stripling. However, these monstrosities, as I may justly call them, which gave me so much trouble to vindicate afterwards, both in company and in a new preface to the second edition of that vile romance, have really, since I came to be in a better mind, proved no small comfort to me, since they have been an effectual means of discrediting the whole relation, and saved me the trouble and shame of doing it in print, especially during the life of many of my worthy friends, who, from a real principle of candor and charity, had publicly engaged in my quarrel, and to whom such an open acknowledgment must have given the greatest mortification; so that though I was come by that time to abhor the imposture, yet I contented myself with owning it only to some of my most intimate friends; and in other company, when questioned about it, with turning the subject in such manner as should give them to understand, that I was ashamed to enter farther into it.

The first edition had not been long published before it was all sold, and a new one demanded, with such alterations and vindication of the old one as might most likely promote the sale, and satisfy at once the curiosity of the public, and the avarice of the proprietor; for, as to me, I had only the small sum of ten guineas for the copy of the first, and twelve more for the improvements in the second, besides such presents as were made me by the generous few to whom I presented them. But before I ventured on the second, I was sent by the good bishop of

London, and my other friends, to Oxford, to pursue such studies as I was fit for, or inclined to, whilst my opposers and advocates were disputing here about the merit or demerit of the first. And when I came to the university, I found many learned and worthy friends as warmly engaged for, as others were against me; and with this seeming advantage on my side, at which I have had frequent occasion to blush, that the former were men of the best character for candor and probity, as well as learning and parts, and whom, for that very reason, I forbear, as I ought, to name, their partiality for me being the mere effect of too extensive a charity and generosity, and which only exposed them to the sarcasms and ridicule of my opponents.

However that be, I had a convenient apartment assigned me in one of the most considerable colleges by the worthy head of it, a man in high reputation for his writings and universal skill in all polite literature, and esteemed one of the most accomplished gentlemen of his age. I was not, indeed, immatriculated, for reasons scarce worth troubling the world with, but had all the other advantages of learning which that college or the university could afford me, either by access to the public and private libraries, or by acquaintance with some of the learned in several other colleges as well as our own, and in this last I had, moreover, a very worthy and learned tutor assigned me, who not only gave me leave to assist at all the lectures he read to his other pupils, some of whom were gentlemen of high birth and fortune, and greatly advanced in learning, but allowed, and even invited me to make such objections as my mind suggested to me, or even to chuse the subject of our entertainment, whether the Newtonian philosophy, logic, poetry, or divinity; which last was, of all others, my favourite one, as well as in a great measure his, for he took orders soon after I left Oxford.

As to the mathematics, in which he was also well skilled, though

I had a great opinion of that study, yet could I never be prevailed to go over the threshold; and the needless demonstrations, as I then thought them, to many of Euclid's propositions, which appeared to me self-evident, such as that the lines that are drawn through a circle, are longer or shorter according to their nearness or distance from the centre, and others of the like nature, seemed to me rather trifling than serious or useful, and I could never have the patience to be better informed. History, especially ancient chronology, &c. appeared so dark, intricate and liable to such unsurmountable difficulties, that I never expected to meet with any satisfaction in them, worth the time and pains they would cost to learn, so that I was a long while before I could be induced to read Scripture history, neither did I begin to be conversant in it till I came to have a taste for the Hebrew tongue, which was not till many years after, and that by mere accident, as I shall shew in the sequel. Church music, which was then in great perfection by the encouragement which the worthy dean of Christ-Church gave it, as well as by several of his excellent compositions in that kind, was the main thing that captivated my vain roving fancy, and took up most of my spare hours, though I was not a little ashamed to see what drunken, idle ragamuffians composed almost every choir there, and with what indolence, to call it by no worse a name, they performed their parts, except on some more solemn occasions than ordinary, as when the bishop, or some persons of distinction, appeared at the Divine worship. The evening I commonly spent with some select company, but without drinking to excess, or even to a degree of exhilaration, which I neither wanted nor was inclined to, and at the usual hour of nine retired to my apartment. But here to make a shew, at least, of retrieving the time I wasted abroad in the day-time in company, music, &c. I used to light a candle, and let it burn the greatest part of the night in my study, to make my neighbours believe I was plying of my books; and sleeping in my easy chair, left the bed often for a whole week as I found it, to the great surprize of my bed-maker, who could hardly imagine how I could live with so little sleep, and without the usual benefit of bed refreshment. Had I not been blessed with a strong constitution, seasoned moreover by two years fatigues in the army, and by my living moderate and low, I might perhaps have felt the sad effects of such an irregularity, and I don't know but my apprehension of it might be one main motive that induced me to make a shew of it, in order to give it the greater merit; for I began to pretend to have swelled legs and feet, and a gouty kind of distemper, which my friends failed not to attribute to that, and earnestly intreated me to submit to more regular hours and method of rest. They likewise prevailed upon me to go and drink some medicinal waters at a small distance from the city, it being then the season, and a good deal of company of both sexes resorting to it; but as I knew myself to stand in no need of any of those helps, I went thither only twice or thrice, rather for the sake of the company, diversion, and music; but as my pretended lameness gave me a kind of gravity, which I was not willing to part with, not knowing how to keep up to the one without the other, I went still limping about like an old gouty fellow, though no man could enjoy a better share of health and flow of spirits than I did all the time I staid there.

It were a shame for me to tell how idly I spent most of my time, and how little progress I made in such a place, company, and among such noble libraries, and learned acquaintance; for, excepting those lectures which I heard from my tutor, most of what I got was by conversation, but little or nothing by reading, except in books of controversy, almost the only ones that could captivate my roving mind. However, it was during my short abode here, (scarcely six months) that I employed my leisure hours in correcting and revising my romance of Formosa, and wrote the best answer I could to the objections that had been made to the first edition, in a second preface, which, all things considered, met with much greater approbation than it deserved, from those few intimates I had shewed it to; after which, taking my leave of all my friends there, I set out for London, where I soon after published that second edition. At my coming to my old lodgings in Pall-Mall, where Dr. Innes and I had formerly lodged, I was told that he was gone over chaplain-general to the English forces in Portugal. I had no reason to regret his absence, for he had, before I went to Oxford, been guilty of such notorious and barefaced immoralities, as well in this as in a former lodging in the Strand, both those of sober and reputable families, that his character had greatly suffered by it, and he went away, just time enough to save himself the mortification of being shamefully turned out of this last, as he had been out of the former. Had I been, indeed, a real convert from heathenism to Christianity, it might have been truly said of him, what our Divine Master said of the Pharisees, compassing sea and land to gain a proselyte, and making him ten times more wicked than themselves; and he hath been more than once severely reproved by his acquaintance, for the scandalous example he gave to me in particular, who was admired by them for the contrary virtues. The truth is, he had an almost insurmountable propensity to wine and women, and when fraught with the former, fell immoderately foul on the latter, whether maids or married, not scrupling to use even violence; which I particularly mention, because his behaviour in these, and several other respects, to say nothing of what I have hinted in a former note, gave me but too much cause to think that he had no real regard to religion, either natural or revealed; so that had I not been happily restrained by Divine Grace, his example would not have failed to have extinguished all sense of remorse which accompanied every indirect action I did, and confirmed me in downright infidelity, in which case I might never have been so happily made sensible of the error of my ways, as I have since been, nor ever repented of them, till it had been too late. I have therefore great reason to acknowledge it the greatest mercy that could befal me, that I was so well grounded in the principles and evidence of the Christian religion, that neither the conversation of the then freethinkers, as they loved to stile themselves, and by many of whom I was severely attacked, nor the writings of a Hobbs, Spinosa, Toland, Collins, Tindal, &c. against the truth of Divine revelation, could appear to me in any other light than as the vain efforts of a dangerous set of men to overturn a religion, the best founded, and most judiciously calculated to promote the peace and happiness of mankind, both temporal and eternal; I must own, that the sophistry which perpetually runs thro' their writings, like the warp through the woof, gave me but too much cause to suspect their sincerity, and that the inveteracy they shew against the noblest system of morality that ever could be thought of, to which all their united force could never substitute any thing better, or near so good, is but a sorry proof of their pretended love to truth, and to the good of mankind, especially when I considered how fully and frequently their writings have been answered and exploded by better hands, without any other visible effect than that of their trumping up the same old trite arguments in some new dress, and claiming a fresh victory from them.

I hope that what I have now wrote will not be deemed by the candid at least, as designed to proclaim my own praise, seeing it rather aggravates my guilt that I could act such a notorious piece of hypocrisy, contrary to the strongest convictions I then felt, that it was impious and offensive to God. What I chiefly mention it here for, is only to observe, that it was that very conviction (which his good providence would not suffer to be quite extinguished in me, though he permitted it to be so long kept under by the impetuosity of my wild and ungovernable vanity) that did at length co-operate with his grace to work in me an utter abhorrence both against that vile and dangerous passion, and the still viler crimes it had involved me in: for if sincerity is one of the most essential virtues of the gospel, how abominable must such a long-winded and multifarious dissimulation appear to a guilty person, when brought to a deep sense of it, however light it might seem to him in the more youthful and inconsiderate part of his life? Those only who have felt can judge of the smart and horror of it, under which nothing could well support them but a sure reliance on the death and merits of a Divine Saviour, and a sincere repentance for, and detestation of it. For as such a happy change can only be the work of Divine Grace, so it gives one a moral and comfortable assurance of pardon and acceptance at the throne of infinite mercy, through the efficacious intercession of our common Redeemer and eternal High Priest.

But though I occasionally mention it here, I would not have it inferred from thence, that I began so soon to give way to so salutary a remorse. I was too young, vain, rash and thoughtless to be any other way influenced by it, than as it put me upon finding out the most senseless excuses and palliatives, such as every one may easily guess at, that hath been, like me, a slave to youthful passions. So that above half a score or a dozen years were mis-spent in a course of the most shameful idleness, vanity and extravagance; some sort of gallantry with the fair sex, with many of whom, even persons of fortune and character of sense, wit, and learning, I was become a great favourite, and might, if I could have overcome my natural sheepishness and fear of a repulse, have been more successful either by way of matrimony or intrigue; which I have since the more wondered at, considering my great propensity to women was as strong as my vanity, and the opportunities so many and inviting, and I so little scrupulous about the danger or guilt of them; yet I may truly say, that hardly any man who might have enjoyed so great a variety, ever indulged himself in so few instances of the unlawful kind as I have done. This I am far from hinting by way of pretence to a greater degree of virtue, of which no man could then have a less share than I; for in those few, wherein I was unhappily engaged, but especially one wherein my effection was captivated to an immoderate degree, no man pursued them with more eagerness and excess than I did. But I am far enough from being inclined to entertain my reader with a detail of my sad irregularities and follies, either in this or other respects, which I have long since looked back upon with shame and sorrow; only, with regard to such kind of unlawful amours, I cannot recal to mind my strong and vehement bias for them, without thankfully acknowledging that there must have been some secret providence that kept me from giving such way as I might otherwise have done to the ruin of my health, circumstances, &c. or my being unwarily drawn into some unhappy marriage, or other snares, into which I have observed many a one less rash, extravagant, and inconsiderate than I, have so unhappily fallen into.

I was led into this sense of God's divine providence towards me, by some (I may say) unavoidable observations on his gracious dispensations, in which it was impossible for me to be mistaken: one was, my meeting with an almost constant disappointment in my most pleasing prospects, my most sanguine expectations and favourite projects, whenever the end proposed was the satisfaction of my predominant passion, or the means to attain it were such as my conscience condemned as unlawful; so that I seldom failed of reaping some pungent shame, mortification or disgrace, where I expected approbation and applause, or with losses and poverty, where I looked for profit or gain. On the other hand, whenever I chearfully entered into any laudable method of living that offered itself, or rather, which the same good Providence threw in my way, I always met with surprising success, and with such credit and approbation as made me ample amends for the struggles my pride made against it on account of its meanness. I shall take the liberty of giving a signal instance, because it hath an immediate connection with the imposture I was still striving to carry on, and consequently deserves to be exposed.

I had been about five or six years in England, and lived in such an extravagant and careless manner (if not in expences, which were rather moderate than lavish, had I been in any laudable way of gaining a competency, but which for want of that often run me into debt, without any visible way of extricating myself) when a plausible way was offered to me, by one Pattenden, of getting money, and credit too, by a white sort of Japan which he had found out, and was then, in vain, endeavouring to recommend to the world, tho' it was really a curious sort of work. His proposal was, that I should father, and introduce it, under the notion of my having learned and brought the art from Formosa; on which condition, and my putting now and then a hand to the painting, he offered me a considerable share in the profit. I readily agreed to his proposal, not only on account of the profit we supposed it would bring, but much more so as it would yield a kind of convincing proof to the fabulous account I had given of myself. We accordingly advertised it under the name of White Formosan Work; and it was viewed and greatly admired by the curious for its fine whiteness, smoothness, and hardness, and for the beauty of the other colours painted upon it: notwithstanding which, and all the extravagant encomiums we gave it, by far beyond what it really deserved, and our care and artifice to conceal its real faults, for some it had, we could never make it succeed so as to be gainers by it. And though our disappointment might be owing, in some measure, to the vast high price he rated it at, contrary to my opinion, yet I have cause to bless God it so happily miscarried, and was forced to quit it; for had the project succeeded according to my sanguine hopes, it would have hardened me only the more irretrievably in my vile imposture and self-conceit, but its being so unaccountably blasted, in spite of all our endeavours to push it forward, did not a little contribute to inspire me with a dislike to all such unlawful and dishonest ways of getting of money, though this was not the immediate result of my disappointment; on the contrary, I grieved at it, and at some other of the like nature, for some years, till the frequency of them made me see clearly into the true cause of them, and fully persuaded me that nothing but an honest and sincere intention, followed by the use of right and lawful means, could be attended with success; for I attempted since then several other means of getting of money, which, though not equally odious as this, were still blameable in me, by reason of my incapacity for them, such as the practising a kind of empyrical physic, teaching of some modern languages, &c. of which I neither was a sufficient master, nor capable of a competent application to make myself so. However, as I was happily disappointed in them all, and as I had reason to think justly too, it set me, at length, on a more honest and laudable scent; and it was not long before Providence threw That in my way, which neither my pride nor my reluctance to a close application, would have suffered me to have sought after, or even thought of: for a counsellor of Lincoln's-Inn, who brought up his three sons and a daughter under his own eye, and had a better opinion of me by far than I deserved, sent for me, and proposed to me the instructing his sons in the Latin tongue, and such other branches of learning, as I should think them capable of, at his own chambers. I readily accepted the offer, notwithstanding the salary was rather too small for the charge, as I was to attend them twice a day, and spend, at least, three hours with them every day, and lived at some distance from him. I was, in about a year's time, honourably discharged, upon his sending them to be farther educated beyond sea.

Soon after this I was recommended to be tutor to a young gentleman, about eight miles from London: his father, who was an officer in the army, had kept him for several years at some considerable schools to little purpose, for when I came to him, he could hardly translate one line out of the plainest Latin authors, which he attributing rather to the remissness of his former masters, than to his want of genius, resolved to give him a home education. I found him, however, so unacquainted with every grammar rule, and so averse to begin afresh with it, he being then near fifteen years of age, that I was obliged to acquaint his father with the little hopes I had of him in the literary way, and proposed the teaching him some other branches of learning, for which he shewed a readier genius, and particularly fortification, which, as I formerly hinted, I had learned from our indolent Jesuit, and of which I was become a pretty good master, by conversation in the army, by seeing a good number of considerable fortresses in several parts of Europe, and more particularly by reading Vauban, Cohorn, and other eminent authors on the subject. My proposal was readily agreed to both by father and son, and the latter made a considerable progress in it in a little time, insomuch that we had not only gone through all the theory of it, and he could take any plan of a place, but had likewise made a model in clay of a large fortified city, in which I had contrived to have a specimen of every thing that related to the art of fortifying, both in the regular and irregular way, engineering, &c. and which, when finished, was not a little admired, not only as a novelty, but likewise as a compleat piece of fortification. The misfortune was, that my salary was neither answerable, as I thought, to the pains I took with my pupil (whom I still made, at proper times, apply himself to Latin, and other branches of literature) but likewise, through the extravagance of the father, very ill paid; which made me so much the more uneasy, as I had contracted some debts which I should have been glad then to have paid with it. This, at length, determined me before the year was quite out, to accept of an offer, which not only appeared more advantageous, but likewise more suitable to my vanity, though it so far disobliged the gentleman's father, that he made no scruple to refuse paying me what was still due to me, and to let me go from him with visible tokens of his resentment.

This happened just after the rebellion was broke out in Lancashire and Scotland, anno 1715, on which account new troops were raised every where, and he became so considerable and flush of money, that I might have made my own terms to have staid with him. But, by that time, some of my friends had prevailed upon the major of a regiment of dragoons, to make me the offer of being clerk to the regiment, and as I knew him to be by far a much finer, and more generous gentleman of the two, nothing could dissuade me from accepting it. He could not, however, prevail on the other captains to make me clerk to their troops, that being, as they said, a perquisite belonging to the quarter-master; but it did not hinder him from retaining me to this, and making such additions to the common salary out of his own pocket, as made it near an equivalent, and the friendship and regard he shewed me, made me be looked upon as a fit companion to the rest of the officers, several of whom having had a liberal education at some of the universities, it was not long before we came into a kind of intimacy; there was, besides, another thing, which procured me no small esteem among them,

viz. my becoming very soon acquainted with the clergy and
other gentlemen in every place we came to, especially with the
learned and curious, by which means I could introduce such of
our officers to them as were men of merit or character, as the most
part of them were. But what added still more weight to the rest
was, that my friend, the major, who had often heard me called
by the familiar nick-name of Sir George, in some of the families
where he had become acquainted with me, after the peace of
Utrecht, took it into his head not only to continue the same stile
to me, but even to give it out, that I had been knighted by queen
Anne. This last I was indeed wholly ignorant of, for a long while,
and denied it as often as the question was put to me, but was,
however, so fond of the feather in the fool's cap, that rather than
forego it, I used to lay a stronger claim to it, under pretence of
my birth and family, for I still passed current for a Formosan, and
was as proud as ever of being thought so, as it procured me such
an access among persons of rank and learning, which I likewise
made a means of bringing our officers and them into a familiar
and agreeable acquaintance, who might otherwise have been
more than ordinarily shy of each other at that critical juncture.
I might add, that as I was likewise a greater favourite of the fair
sex, than any of the red coats, whom they could not but look
upon with some dread at that time, I had frequent invitations
from them, even those of rank and fortune, whose curiosity
would not permit them to suffer so great a stranger as I was to
come, or even to pass so near them, without having the pleasure
of seeing and conversing with him, and informing themselves
in all the particulars that related to him. And as I always took
care to behave in such a manner as might gain their esteem, as
well as admiration, so I could the more easily introduce such of
our gentlemen as bore an unexceptionable character to them,
by which means we had the satisfaction of spending many a

pleasant day in their company in the most innocent and agreeable manner, particularly in Lancashire, and, after the suppression of the rebellion, where we continued quarters, at Wigan, Warrington and Manchester, in which last I had, moreover, the opportunity of frequently visiting a noble library belonging to the collegiate church, and well furnished with all manner of books that could be purchased with money: for it is endowed with 100l. per ann. to supply it with new ones as they come out, and yet, when I was there, they had above 500l. in bank, and scarce knew how to lay it out, insomuch that they were thinking of purchasing of some of the most curious manuscripts. This, I could not but observe to them, was ill judged, considering the situation of it, chiefly among tradesmen, who have neither taste nor knowledge of such valuable pieces, and the few learned men in that neighbourhood that could reap any benefit from them, and rather advised them to lay out that income in purchasing such valuable modern books, as were yearly published both in England and out of it, and which, I thought, would better answer the intention of the noble donor. They seemed to acquiesce in what I said; but whether they followed my advice or not, I never enquired since.

These allurements, so soothing to my natural vanity, and our often moving from one county to another, made me stay longer in the regiment than I ought in reason or conscience (had I been capable of listening to either) to have done, considering that I was of no service, but only a dead weight to my friend the major, who, being moreover as bad an oeconomist as myself, would have been glad enough to have been rid of me, though he never, either in word or carriage, gave me the least hint of it, but rather the contrary; yet some of those friends of mine, who had recommended me to him at first, had more than once advised me to ease him of so expensive a load; yet so pleased was I with this wandering and idle kind of life, which gave me an opportunity of travelling through, and seeing, so many countries I should otherwise never have been able to see, that I could not prevail upon myself to leave the regiment, till it was ordered into Ireland, and then marched as far as Bristol with them, and saw them embarked for that kingdom: so that I had been, from first to last, somewhat above two years in this wandering kind of amusing life, without reaping any other advantage than the seeing variety of places and people, and conversing here and there with some learned men and books, though nothing so much with the latter as I might have done, if my indolence, vanity and the variety of objects which danced before my eyes, had not diverted me from it.

Upon my return from Bristol, I was at no small loss how to dispose of myself for some time, and having had time to ruminate upon my mis-spent time and idle life, was easily induced, by some of my friends, to alter my course, and, if possible, to get into a way of earning a competency by my own industry, rather than live at other people's cost, or, which was much worse, on their charity, which I could not now but look upon myself as a most unworthy object of; and, as I had a little smattering of painting and drawing, and had I been capable of a proper application, might, with assistance, have attained to a considerable proficiency in it, having a strong genius for, and no indifferent judgment in it. However, to go the nearest and easiest way to work, I resolved on that of fan painting, which required less time and pains to learn; and had the profit been any thing answerable to my assiduity, I could have been contented to have drudged on with it still. But that business was then at so low and contemptible an ebb, that, though I lived with a good family almost gratis, and was early and late at work, yet I found it impossible to get a bare competency by it; notwithstanding the

encouragement several of my friends and acquaintance gave me.
This, however, brought me acquainted with a worthy clergyman;
who, thinking the employment too mean for a man of my
education and parts, and that I might bestow my time to much
better purpose in some kind of laudable study, particularly that
of divinity, which I had always been most fond of and conversant
in, engaged to raise a subscription among his acquaintance, by
which I might be enabled to follow my studies with more ease.
He did it accordingly, to the amount of between twenty and
thirty pounds per ann. which, with the help of a small addition I
got to it, by perfecting of a young gentleman in the Latin tongue
and some other branches of learning, made it a comfortable
competency, especially as I was become, by this time, a better
oeconomist, and had fallen into a more frugal way of living.

But all this while this subscription did lie somewhat heavy
on my conscience, and at some particular times gave me no
small uneasiness, inasmuch as it was founded on a belief of my
being a Formosan, and a real convert to the church of England,
which those pious subscribers had not any doubt of, that I could
find, even to their dying day; for whenever I waited on them, I
always met with the kindest reception and civil treatment that
could be wished. This uneasiness still increased, as I now and
then met with some people at their houses, whose behaviour
and objections, though not in plain terms, gave me but too
much reason to think they had not the same charitable opinion
of me; and this put me upon various indirect means to prevent
my friends being prevailed upon by them to withdraw their
benevolence. This made me often wish and pray, that I might
but fall into some more honest way of living without it, and
free myself by it from that aggravated remorse, with which I
was forced to receive it. But though I was fully persuaded of the
guilt, yet I was not sensibly enough affected with it to make an

open confession of it, and how unworthy I was of their charitable opinion and assistance; and contented myself with making some resolutions of giving up the latter, at least, as soon as I could get myself into a way of living without it.

I became, at length, providentially I may say, acquainted with a person who was concerned in various branches relating to the printing trade, and in very good circumstances. He was, moreover, a very generous and good-natured gentleman, and I became, in a little time, so great a favourite, that he could scarce pass a day without seeing and consulting me about some of his affairs; and by his means I came at last to translate books, and to get a comfortable living by it. It was then I began to perceive, with no small joy, how God blessed my endeavours in proportion to my diligence and honesty, which made so lively an impression on my mind, that I resolved never to be concerned in any works, that were either prophane, heretical, or of a trifling nature or ill tendency, and have accordingly refused them whenever they have been offered to me. From translating of other people's works, I came at length to print some of my own, and with the same laudable view, and have found still more credit and comfort in it, and more cause to bless the Divine mercy, for the wonderful and undeserved success I have since met with. But of these I shall speak in a more proper place; in the mean time I shall only observe here, that my charitable friends, dying one after another, as my business increased, I never applied to the survivors for a continuance of their benevolence, but declined it where it was offered, as being then able to live without it: and I can only add, that though I once looked upon these subscriptions as no less unworthily bestowed upon, than basely received by me, yet I have had the comfort to observe since, that they proved the happy means of freeing me from a more laborious and unprofitable life, and of enabling me to follow those studies with more ease and chearfulness, which fitted me, in time, for those more arduous and beneficial tasks, which I have been since engaged in; seeing it was during the greater part of that time, that I applied myself to the Hebrew tongue, and to the more close study of the sacred books; by which means I had an opportunity of making a large collection of critical and other remarks, which, though designed then only for my own information, came at length to have a place in one of those works I shall speak of in the sequel, where they have since met with the approbation of the public, both in England and abroad; though even under those encouragements, and with those opportunities I had, I must own, to my shame, that I was still fair enough from such a laudable application, as might have turned them to better advantage; and that I still mis-spent a great deal of my time in a loose, careless manner, and that it was not till after a year or two that I disengaged myself from company, especially of the fair sex, though, one person excepted, rather trifling than culpable, to follow my books more closely. I shall therefore skip all the former part of my time, from the twentieth to the thirty-second year of my age, as a sad blank to every thing that was good or laudable, and fraught with a dismal variety of folly, indiscretion and other miscarriages, which would rather disgust than inform, or even divert a sober reader, to come to a more hopeful and instructive period; and only observe, before-hand, that it was no small happiness to me, (which, to whatsoever owing, I ought at least to attribute to my own discretion) that the many learned and pious persons I was formerly, and continued still, acquainted with, (for it was with such that I mostly chose to converse) were never acquainted with, nor, as I could perceive, ever suspected me of being guilty of such a shameful, idle and scandalous way of living, but believed that I spent most of my time to better purpose; else it is not to be doubted but I had been discarded and shunned by them. In which case I should have entirely lost the most effectual means of coming into a better way of thinking, which their conversation, example, and the many good books which they lent me, did at length happily bring me to, and been left, like a weather-cock, exposed to all winds: for though I could talk, and, at some serious intervals, think as seriously as they of religion and its most important duties, and even comply with them in such a manner, as seemed very delightful and edifying to them; yet was my roving heart so far from joining sincerely, or being affected with them, that I could easily forego them, to indulge any new rising satisfaction, though ever so opposite. And indeed, such a frequent variety did offer itself naturally in my way, as I was in no way able to resist.

Thus, for instance, it was natural for those intimates to introduce or renew some old subject or topic relating to my pretended country, travels, conversion, or other romantic part of my life, which, however irksome it was then become to me to repeat, and as it were to confirm anew; yet there was no way for me to avoid it, unless I had at once acknowledged the whole relation to have been a notorious and shameful imposture; and what a deadly wound must have such an unexpected confession given to my natural vanity? and what a mortification would it have been, to such sincere honest people, to hear it from my own mouth? so that, could I even have had courage enough to forego the former, as I have more than once thought and even resolved to do, yet how could I find it in my heart to give so sensible a displeasure to persons that had shewn so much friendship and zeal for me? to say nothing of the dreadful apprehensions of the consequence of their charitable opinion being thereby turned into a just abhorrence and detestation. This was the sad dilemma I found myself in when I came to reflect seriously on my case, and which made me conclude it, all things considered, altogether impossible for me to extricate myself out of, without some miraculous power to assist me to overcome a passion, which had hitherto eluded all the opposition which my reason and experience had been able to raise against it. But what glimpse of hope of any such Divine help could such a wretch have, who, with his eyes open to the guilt and danger, had brought himself into such a dangerous state? But God's mercy, which is over all his works, is not to be judged of by us according to our narrow apprehensions, but according to the gracious manifestation he has given us of it in his gospel; and as that assurance gave me good grounds to hope, so that hope inspired me with a design to use all proper means to obtain it, and leave the issue of it to his Divine Providence. To him, therefore, I thankfully give all the praise for his undeserved and singular blessing on those means which himself directed me to, and what the chiefest of them were I have already mentioned, and shall take notice of some others in the sequel, in hopes they may prove of service to such as may stand in the same need of them as I did then.

However, I must own, that the resolution had something awful and deterring, when I considered it in its full extent, to exchange the delights of variety and multiplicity of company (which had been so delightful and insnaring to me till then, that no motive or obstacle could keep me from it) for solitude and retirement; their bewitching flatteries and commendations, whether for a false merit I had assumed, or for some valuable things they fancied in me, for a closer recollection and abhorrence of my own vileness; to spending of so much precious time in the gaities and guilty vanities of life, for a more close application and search after the properest and most effectual means of redeeming that invaluable jewel, and the parcelling and bestowing it to the most beneficial purposes; to retrench not only all unnecessary and unlawful expences, but even some of the common and necessary ones, in order to make some amends for past extravagancies, by supplying the wants of those many objects, that used to pass by unobserved and unpitied by me.

These, and other such like indispensable preparatives, to the desired thorough change, seemed to carry such unsurmountable difficulties with them, that neither my small share of reason nor philosophy could have supported me to any tolerable degree in the resolutions I was daily striving to make after it. And indeed, nothing so effectually did it, as the consideration that that Divine Providence, which had inspired me with that desire, would not fail of compleating it, if I was not wanting to myself; for that at once set me upon trying sometimes one, sometimes another, of those duties, with success enough at least to encourage me to proceed.

And here I was again providentially helped by a worthy clergyman at Braintree in Essex; who, good man, had a much better opinion of me than I deserved, and presented me with that excellent book called Reformed devotions, and recommended by the late reverend Dr. Hicks. This excellent book, though then unknown to me, and disrelished by some weak Christians, is so well known to all the true devout ones, that I need say no more in commendation of it, than that it proved of such vast benefit to me, that I can never sufficiently admire it, or the piety of the compiler and reformer; for the many opportunities and invitations it gives one of frequent and closer intercourse with God, and of meditating, in the most exalted manner, on his various works, infinite mercies, and on all the sublime truths and duties of Christianity, did so effectually reconcile me to that solitude and retirement I had formerly been so averse to, and afforded me a most noble refreshment several times a day, from my close application to other studies I was then pursuing, some of which being of the dry, others of the complex kind, might have

gone but sluggishly on without it. The late pious Mr. Nelson's
Method of Devotion falling likewise, soon after, into my hands,
in order to be conveyed, by my means, to a young gentlewoman
lately recovered from a state of despondency, I had the curiosity
to run through it, and found in it such excellent, yet easy rules for
the conquering of our natural vices, and recovering the contrary
virtues to them, that I made it one of my daily monitors, and
with no small success.

But that which gave me the greatest help, was the learned
and pious Mr. Law's Serious Call to Devotion. This truly
valuable treatise I accidentally found on a clergyman's table,
who, nevertheless, soon took it out of my hand, and gave such
a character of it, as might have discouraged me from looking
farther into it, had not the place I had opened given me a quite
different notion of it. However, as I could not prevail upon him to
lend it me, I went and bought me one, and read it over and over,
from beginning to end, with greater eagerness and satisfaction
than any I had ever met with on that subject. I was particularly
much taken with the author's motives, as well as his method for
the right use of our time, money, talents, &c. not to mention that
his variety of characters and reasonings upon them, which are a
continued appeal to the most unbiassed and soundest judgement,
which admit of neither cavil or objection, soon opened to me
a much better way of applying them to advantage, than any I
had hitherto, or could indeed have fallen into, without such an
excellent guide. The directions he gives for the obtaining of those
Christian virtues, which he there recommends as the proper
subject for the several hours of prayer in the day, may indeed
appear to have something too technical (since it is no other than a
daily renewing of those very desires, till themselves become the
virtues we want) from which too much of the success may, by the
light and thoughtless, be ascribed to the method, and too little

to the grace of God accompanying it. For may not, some will be apt to say, an honest heathen or deist, by the same method, raise himself up into a habit of sobriety, chastity, &c. without any such application to, or particular assistance from, the Supreme Being? yet let any serious person try the efficacy of it against any of his favourite, especially his constitutional vices, and he will find, at length, that he hath been only trying to wash a Blackmoor white, and must do so to the end of the chapter, without the intervention of Divine grace. As for me I shall always, I hope, look upon the desire itself, as well as the success of the means used for the obtaining any virtue, to be alike the work of God in the soul, let these be such as Mr. Law directs, or any other, which Providence puts into our hands.

I had long before this, however, began to consecrate part of my time to the study of the sacred books, tho' not in that regular and uniform manner as I happily fell into after reading the excellent directory above mentioned, and had made a pretty collection of criticisms, and other observations upon them, such as occurred on my reading of the various commentators on them; and now it was that I became sensible, indeed, of my own want of knowledge of the original Hebrew, and to bewail the loss of several opportunities I had missed of gaining a more perfect knowledge in that sacred and useful tongue. For I had been so discouraged from the pursuit of it, by the difficulties I met with at the very threshold, that is, in the grammars, that I never had the patience to go thro' one of them, but contented myself with the interliniary versions of Pagninus, Arias Montanus, and other Interpreters; chusing rather to rely on their honesty and skill, than to be at the trouble of becoming a proper judge of either. It was not indeed possible for me to go on long in this groping way, before their various interpretations of the text, (especially those of some bold critics, which seemed calculated to unhinge, rather than confirm our belief, by exploding several, till then, acknowledged facts and doctrines, or interpreting them in their own artful way) set me again upon making some fresh efforts, for attaining a more perfect knowledge of the original, which were however soon damped by every fresh difficulty I met with in the common way of learning it, till I providentially stumbled, as it were, on the following easy method.

I was then hammering at an exercitation on the 34th Psalm, printed at the end of the grammar that goes under the name of Bellarmine; in which I found at almost every word some exceptions to the grammar rules, and such reasons assigned for them as still carried one farther from the point in view; when a poor man came and offered me a pocket Hebrew psalter, with Leusden's Latin version, over against each page. I greedily bought it, and finding the version much more easy and natural than those literal ones of Pagninus and Montanus, quickly went through every verse in the book, without troubling myself about grammar, or any thing but the true meaning of every word as they occurred. So that by the time I had given it a second reading, my memory being the best faculty I could boast of, I had by that very rote, as I may call it, not only gained a considerable copia verborum, but by observation on the flexion of nouns, verbs, &c. got a tolerable insight into the declensions, conjugations, and other parts of the grammar and syntax; and, whenever any difficulty or doubt occurred, could easily turn to my Bellarmine or even Buxstorf, the most discouraging of all; because, having then but one point in view, I could, without perplexing my mind with any more than that, either satisfy myself about it, or at the worst postpone it, till a further reading and observation brought me to it: I became so fond of this method, that having gone through a third reading of it, with little or no obstacle, and in a very little time, I resolved thenceforth to confine myself to the psalms of each day, as they are read at church, and to begin with the historical books.

Here, instead of perplexing myself with such Bibles as had the servile letters printed in a different kind of character, to distinguish them from the radicals, I pitched upon the first edition of that of Munster, which is far inferior to the second, and, by the help of his version on the opposite column, though often at several lines distance from the original, had hardly gone through six or eight chapters of the first book of Samuel, before the ease I found in it invited me to go back to Genesis, and take every chapter in its course. I resolved at first to run them over once, without taking notice of his notes, because the greatest part of them were either of the Massoretic or of the Cabbalistical kind, and would rather clog than assist; and even in these of the grammatical sort he lays all along so great a stress on the punctuation for the true meaning and import of each word, as made his version the less to be depended upon. For though I always did and do still look upon the points to be of singular help to learners, and consequently on the method proposed by some moderns of teaching the Hebrew without them, as wild, intricate, and in some cases dangerous, yet from all I had been able to gather from the learned authors who have wrote on the controversy, I was so far from thinking them of the same authority with the text, they plainly appeared of too modern a date to be used in any other shape than as an expeditious help; and as such I still made use of them, without confining myself to them any farther than they were supported by the dialect, by the ancient paraphrases and versions, and other such critical helps, but made no scruple to depart from them whenever a small change of them could afford one a clearer or better sense. And for that I shall refer the reader to what I have since wrote on that so much controverted subject in the Jewish history, which makes the seventh chapter of the Universal History, and especially in the folio edition, where I had more room to expatiate upon it than in the octavo one, in which our being confined to reduce the whole within the compass of twenty volumes, obliged us to be a little more concise. I must therefore here own with pleasure, that all that I there advanced hath been so well received, and looked upon as so well grounded, that it hath not, that I know of, been since censured or contradicted; and that though the controversy in favour of the antiquity and authority of the points hath been of late revived with no small warmth, I have met with nothing in it, nor heard from either those I converse or correspond with, any thing that could give me cause to alter my mind. I shall only beg leave to add, that my looking on the Hebrew points, both vowel and gramatical only in that view, enabled me to make many useful discoveries in the sacred books, which have been highly approved by those who have since read them in the history abovementioned.

But to return to my first reading of the original books, I ran with ease through the Pentaeuch, Joshua, Judges, &c. except the few poetical parts which occur in it, such as Exod. xv. pass. Deut. xxxii. Judges v. .1 Samuel ii. 1-10. where the stile is not only swoln and figurative, but where the construction is harsh, irregular, and to appearance truncated, and several terms which occur no where else; so that finding them too hard for me to surmount, with all the application I had, I postponed them to a future reading. I found likewise pretty near the same difficulty in the Proverbs, Ecclesiastes, and the Song of Solomon, and much more still in Job; and therefore contented myself with catching as much as I could at one cursory reading, and leaving the rest for hereafter; yet did not this discourage me from going through all the Prophets in course, though it proved an arduous task, and I went but slowly on, because in these I endeavoured to make myself as much master of their meaning and stile, as well as of the new words and phrases peculiar to them: and as I spent generally some hours a day on that study, I had quickly gone through all the sacred books of the Old Testament, excepting those chapters in Daniel, Ezra, &c. which are in the Chaldee, and where I contented myself at this first reading, with examining as well as I was able, the difference between that and the Hebrew. And here I own I found such a disparity between them, such a noble simplicity, and yet masculine energy in the latter, and such an apparent softness and effeminacy in the former, not unlike what is justly observed between Latin and Italian, that I believe nothing could have tempted me to become more acquainted with it, had it not been for the vast helps which the Chaldee paraphrase affords us, not only in fixing the meaning of many obscure words and expressions, but, what is still more valuable, in discovering the sentiments of the ancient Jews concerning many pregnant prophecies of the Messiah, from which the Talmudic writers have since departed out of dislike to him.

When I came to the second reading of Genesis, by which time I had likewise ran through the Psalms five or six times, and was got again into the historical stile, I found myself so unclogged, so acquainted with the grammar and syntax, and master of such a vast number of words, that I began to think I might begin to read the Latin into Hebrew; that is, by hiding the Hebrew column with my hand, try how I could make my own agree to it. This I found however too hard and tedious, except in some easy places or chapters, and I found myself not only at a loss for the words, but mostly in the conjugating and syntax, and though it might in all likelihood have quitted cost, had I proceeded regularly in that method, yet I found it too tedious, as it took me above twice the time, so that I contented myself with only trying it now and then, when the humour took, or the subject invited me to it. At other

leisure times, I used likewise to exercise myself in conjugating of
verbs by dint of memory and observation, and then to compare
it with those in the grammar, by which I soon found out wherein
I was deficient, and this I thought more expeditious, diverting,
and effectual, than the dull method of beginners, who, by dint
of hammering, learn them by heart, scarcely knowing what they
are about. One thing however I found would be a great help, viz.
in all dubious words, as the Hebrew is so figurative and scanty,
to have recourse to the Lexicon, in order to find out the primitive
sense of them from the more remote, which it was easy to do
by the parallel texts there pointed at, where they occurred. This
method duely attended to, opens a spacious insight into the true
meaning of the sacred books. Thus I found for instance in the
words רוח אלהים מרחפת Genesis i. 2. the spirit of God moved
upon the face of the waters, compared with the motion of the
eagle in stirring her young ones to flight, Deut. xxxii. 11. that
the verb רדף in the former in its primitive sense, is not such
a motion as our version expresses, nor a brooding like that of
the hen over her eggs, as some other translations intimate, but
a lively agitation, such as much better explains the action of the
spirit of God upon the face of the waters. This method, which
I preferred to the consulting that variety of versions we have,
which rather confound than fix the sense, inabled me in my very
second going through the sacred books, to make a pretty large
collection of such kind of criticisms and observations, as have
been since of singular use to me in the progress of my study,
and in some of those works in which I have been since engaged,
though I little thought then either they, or those which I made
out of other authors that came in my way, would ever come into
public view.

I had by this time made so great a proficiency in the Hebrew,
tongue that I could have talked it pretty fluently, had I been as

well acquainted with the pronunciation of it. But as that could not be attained from grammars, which differed almost as much in the rules they gave for it, as the native languages of their authors differed from each other, I thought it might be more easily attained by conversing with the Jews themselves, going to their synagogues, and hearing the Scriptures read by their chazans or ministers, who, I supposed, were perfect masters of it. But here, to my great surprise, I found that they not only greatly differed among themselves, that is, the northern from the southern, or German, Polish, Hungarian, &c. from the Spanish, Portuguese, Italian, &c. but that every one of them pronounced it after the same manner as they did the languages of the countries where they had been brought up, and, as it plainly appeared to me, none of them right. And this was farther confirmed to me by conversing with some Morocco Jews, whose native language being the Arabic, made me think they bid fairest for having retained the antient pronunciation in a greater degree at least of purity; for some of them whom I met with by chance in the Portuguese synagogue, made a mere ridicule of their way of reading and pronouncing it. And it was by conversing with some of these, who were besides well acquainted with the Hebrew, that I took my rules for a more genuine way of speaking it: and it was no small pleasure to me to find, that I could be very readily understood by all the southern Jews, though I could not so easily understand them, on account of their not sufficiently distinguishing between the sounding of sundry consonants, aspirations, gutturals, &c. which seemed to me to have originally differed very greatly; such as the שׁ and שׂ and ס the קבּ and ח the הע and א the טּ ו and צ &c. but between which they do not make any distinction, nor indeed can, for want of having been taught it in their youth. In the same manner do they murder it, when they go about to write it in European characters, witness that Spanish dialogue of the famed

R. Netto, intituled אש דת esh dath, the legal fire, but which he spells, after his Spanish manner of pronouncing, es dat. However, after I had once been fully apprised of all the defects of their reading, which several of them I have conversed with have had the ingenuity to own as such, I could easily enough understand both their lectures of the Old Testament and their prayers. But as to the northern Jews, I own I never could converse with them in that tongue, without an interpreter, or some go-between, who, by the help of travelling into other parts, had learned the way to accomodate their speech to both ways of pronouncing, so much wider and uncooth is theirs to that of the southern; and this was no small grief to me, because I always found the northern more learned and communicative, as well as more fluent and ready at speaking that sacred tongue; though that consideration was never sufficient to induce me to be at the pains to accustom myself to their way. Thus much I thought might be necessary to say with respect to the pronunciation of the Hebrew, to which I shall only add, that my method for learning and preserving it was by reading it aloud to myself, and with the same exactness, as if I had been reading it to an assembly.

But what contributed most to this extraordinary readiness of speaking it, was a method I fell into at proper times, when I found myself inclined to close thinking, to cloath my ideas in that, instead of any other language, or, as one may more properly word it, to think in Hebrew rather than in English, or any other language I was used to. The Psalter, which at my first setting up for this study, I had read over for some time, at least three or four times a month, and afterwards constantly went through once a month ever since, was become so familiar to me, that I had got it by heart; and as that contains most of the radical words, as well as idioms, which are most in use, I seldom was at a loss for either in these my soliloquies, or, if I was, I immediately endeavoured to call to mind where I had read any thing like it, either in that or any other of the sacred books, and by turning to it, if I could not readily recover it by dint of memory, seldom failed of fixing it there indelibly. By this means I soon acquired not only a surprising fluency in it, but could speak it in the pure and elegant stile of the sacred writers, and now and then, upon occasion, raise it to the lofty strain of the poetical books. This I was the more admired for, because it was what few, if any, of the learned among the Jews could do, who commonly marred their own by an heterogeneous mixture of the corrupt Talmudic and Rabbinic words and idioms, to which I was then in a great measure a stranger, nor could ever be reconciled to after I became more acquainted with them. One may, indeed, observe almost the same difference between the former and the latter, some few of these excepted, as there is between the Latin of the Augustin age, and that which was in vogue after the inundation of the northern barbarians into the Roman empire, as the reader may see by what I have said of it in my History of the Jews from their Dispersion after the destruction of Jerusalem to this time.

By what I have said hitherto of my method of learning Hebrew, any one may see how easily men at years of maturity may come to as perfect knowledge of it, as the thing will admit of, and without the discouraging slavery of beginning at the grammar, and may even make that a pleasing relaxation from other studies; and it is with a view of lessening, if not altogether removing those fancied difficulties and discouragements which have been the cause of that sacred tongue being so much, and, I may add, so shamefully neglected, by the clergy especially, that I have ventured to write so far on that subject from my own experience; for, let them think of or palliate it as they will, such a neglect must of necessity be condemned, by all who seriously consider how impossible it is to come at a true knowledge, not only of the Old, but I will be bold to say of the New Testament, without a sufficient knowledge of the Hebrew: the first seems to me self-evident, and with respect to the second, or New Testament, I need only observe, that the writers of it, though inspired, and endowed with the gift of tongues, did visibly adhere still to the Hebrew idiom in which they had been brought up, St. Paul himself not excepted. Hence, the vast quantity of Hebraisms that occur more or less in the Gospels, Acts, and in the Epistles, and which never can be rightly understood or explained, but by having recourse to the Hebrew idiom; but this hath been so fully displayed by much better pens, that I shall say no more on the subject.

I have often wished, indeed, that we had some more inviting helps to that study than we have, and such as might more effectually contribute to overcome the aversion, or indifference, which our young clergy seem to have for it. And in order to contribute something more than a bare wish towards it, I had once gone a good way in composing a tragi-comic piece, intituled, David and Michol, in Hebrew verse, wherein I introduced this young princess, acknowledging with a suitable reluctancy and shame to her confident, her new born affection for the young shepherd, after she had seen him unperceived from behind a curtain in her father's pavilion, and heard some of these inimitable strains with which he was wont to enliven that desponding monarch in his most melancholy hours. The distress arising from the apprehended rivalship of her eldest sister, who was soon after promised as a reward to that brave youth, for killing the vapouring champion of the Philistines and Morabs, being represented here as having already settled her affections on Adriel the Meholathite, to whom Saul actually gave her soon after, contrary to his promise (1 Sam. xviii. 19.) the different fears and emotions of the two sisters, the means by which they came to understand each other's case and inclinations, the singular affection of Jonathan towards David, and the kind offices he did him with Saul, in order to procure him his beloved Michol, instead of her sister; all these, I say, are represented in divers affecting scenes, to which the energy of the Hebrew gives no small beauty and pathos. The Episodes, the most considerable of which consist of several interviews and conferences between the prophet Samuel and young David, as when he acquainted him with Saul's utter rejection, and his being chosen by God to succeed him in the Israelitish kingdom, David's surprise, scruples and fears, his dread of entertaining even the most distant hope of a crown, which he could not obtain but by the most unnatural and blackest treason against his father-in-law, and his most generous friend Jonathan, and the arguments by which the prophet endeavours to satisfy his scrupulous mind, that he shall enjoy the promised crown, without the least stain to his loyalty, and at length prevails on him to suffer himself to be anointed king; these, and some others of less importance, are not improper interludes to bring the piece to its happy catastrophe, his marrying the kind and beloved Michol, and being justly raised to the command of the Israelitish army. To this I had added a literal version, which I designed to have illustrated with critical notes; but some avocations obliged me to set it aside for a considerable number of years, and when I came to give it a fresh reading, I found it to fall so short of the elegance and loftiness of the sacred poets, with whom I was become by that time much better acquainted, and a much greater admirer of, that I was quite discouraged from improving or even finishing, especially when I considered the little likelihood there was of its meeting with encouragement answerable to the pains and cost, at a time when one might observe the study of that tongue to dwindle more and more visibly into contempt, among those whose duty and business it ought to have been to cultivate and promote it.

The same mortifying consideration made me likewise set aside a design I had formed, of compiling some scriptural Hebrew Dialogues, in imitation of the Latin ones of Castalio, and a set of others on more common subjects, like those of Corderius, tho' not so puerile, for the encouragement and diversion of young beginners; and a third between a Jew, and a Christian, on the most material points of controversy between us, together with a collection and exposition of a great number of texts, both in the Old, and New Testament, plainly foretelling the future restoration of the twelve tribes of Israel, to their own Land, and their embracing Christian religion at the second coming of Christ, towards the close of the sixth, or in the beginning of the seventh millenary of the world; for though that doctrine is, as the Jews at Rome said of Christianity, every where spoken against, (Acts, cap. ult. v. 22.) I never found it to be so but by men who, like these Jews had never rightly considered it; whilst those who really have, (among whom I have known several eminent divines of the church of England, and some among the Dissenters who were thoroughly satisfied with it) contented themselves with owning their belief of it to their intimate friends, without daring to preach or promote it, for fear of being reflected or ridiculed for it. But I have had frequent occasion to observe since (vide Jual un Hestor, fol. edit. vol. i. p. 613, &c. 8vo. edit. vol. iii. p. 39. and above all, see the conclusion of their history, from the dispersion to this present time) that the Christians denying that doctrine, is one of the most effectual means not only of hardening the Jews in their unbelief, but of unhinging one of the greatest evidences of the Christian faith, since it cannot be proved in any sense, that any of those glorious prophecies concerning the happy state of the Jews under the Messiah, which are scattered through the Old and New Testament, have been fulfilled; but that, on the contrary, they have for the most part been hated, persecuted and miserable, in most countries in the world, ever since the death of Christ. However, as I had little encouragement to hope that such a subject, written in Hebrew, how beneficial soever it might have proved, at least to young beginners, especially by the help of the Latin version, would relish with the present age, I likewise postponed it for some happier time, which is not yet come, if ever I should live to see it.

I therefore contented myself with preparing for the press a new edition of the Psalms, with Leusden's Latin version over against it, and some critical and other notes for the use of the learners, interspersed here and there, with others of a more curious nature, on several defficient places of that book, and most of them new. To this I designed a preface, that should give an account of the method by which I had, chiefly by the means of the psalms, attained to my knowledge of the Hebrew tongue, in the manner I have lately related. I designed to add some further directions than those I have mentioned, with respect to the more easy attaining a readiness of understanding and speaking it, one of which was, in the frequent reading to change the third into the second person at proper places, and so turning the psalm into a kind of prayer, which, by raising the attention, imprints the words more in the mind, as well as familiarizes the conjugating of the verbs, &c. and this I found a great help to my progress, and was approved by some judges, upon which I acquainted Mr. Palmer, of Bartholomew's Close, one of the best printers then in England, with my design, and was surprised one day on my coming to talk further about it, to hear that the reverend Dr. W — — had been there just before, to treat with him about printing a new edition of it, said to have been compiled by Dr. Hare, since bishop of Chichester, who pretended to have found out the true metre of the Psalms, and by means of that to have made a great number of considerable discoveries and emendations in the original. I knew but too well how many excellent critics had already split upon that fatal rock, and who, instead of correcting, had quite marred the Hebrew, by distorting, transposing and altering it at pleasure, in order to bring it to their model, to expect any thing solid or satisfactory from that quarter, considering especially the character of the author. Nor was I mistaken, though this performance did not appear in print till seven or eight years after, and then to my great surprise. For Mr. Palmer had amused me with the belief that the design was set aside, either on account of its being found impracticable, or at least too difficult and dangerous; for that, upon his applying to Dr. W___ to enquire further about it, he had received such evasive answers, as plainly convinced him, that the author did not design to go on with it, which still confirmed me more in my old opinion, that all attempts to recover the antient metre of the sacred poetical books, were fruitless and lost labour. It appeared however, as I shall show hereafter, that Mr. Palmer imposed upon me, and that he knew that the design was carried on in another printing-house, though with such privacy, that I never heard or dreamed of it, though I had been long acquainted with Mr. Bowyer, who was employed in the printing of it. So far from it was I, that I began to think Mr. Palmer had only invented that story to divert me from printing my proposed edition, in order to set me upon another work, in which he was more immediately concerned, and expected greater credit, as well as present profit from. This was his history of printing, which he had long promised to the world, but for which he was not at all qualified. However, he designed to have added a second part, relating to the practical art, which was more suited to his genius, and in which he designed to have given a full account of all that relates to that branch, from the letter-founding to the most elegant way of printing, imposing, binding, &c. in which he had made considerable improvements of his own, besides those he had taken from foreign authors; but this second part, though but then as it were in embryo, met with such early and strenuous opposition from the respective bodies of letter founders, printers, and bookbinders, under an ill-grounded apprehension, that the discovery of the mystery of those arts, especially the two first, would render them cheap and contemptible (whereas the very reverse would have been the case, they appearing indeed the more curious and worthy our admiration, the better they are known) that he was forced to set it aside. But as to the first part, viz. the history of printing, he met with the greatest encouragement, not only from them, but from a very great number of the learned, who all engaged to subscribe largely to it, particularly the late earls of Pembroke and Oxford, and the famous doctor Mead, whose libraries were to furnish him with the noblest materials for the compiling of it, and did so accordingly.

The misfortune was, that Mr. Palmer, knowing himself unequal to the task, had turned it over to one Papiat, a broken Irish bookseller then in London, of whom he had a great opinion, though still more unqualified for it than he, and only aimed at getting money from him, without ever doing any thing towards it, except amusing him with fair promises for near three quarters of a year. He had so long dallied with him that they were come within three months of the time in which Mr. Palmer had engaged to produce a compleat plan, and a number or two of the first part, by way of specimen of the work, viz. the invention and improvement of it by John Faust at Mentz; and these were to be shewn at a grand meeting of learned men, of which Dr. Mead was president that year, and being his singular friend and patron, was to have promoted a large subscription and payment, which Mr. Palmer stood in great need of at that time. Whereas Papiat had got nothing ready but a few loose and imperfect extracts out of Chevalier la Caille, and some other French authors on the subject, but which could be of little or no use, because he frequently mistook them, and left blanks for the words he did not understand.

These however, such as they were, Mr. Palmer brought to me, and earnestly pressed me that I would set aside all other things I might be then about, and try to produce the expected plan and specimen by the time promised, since he must be ruined both in credit and pocket, if he disappointed his friends of it. It was well for him and me, that the subject lay within so small a compass as the consulting of about twelve or fourteen principal authors, and the controversy between Mentz and Harlem universally decided in favour of the former, so that I easily fell upon a proper plan of the work, which I divided into three parts, the first which was, to give an account of the invention of the art, and its first essays by Faust at Mentz, and of its improvement by fusile or metal types, varnish, ink, &c. by his son-in-law Peter Schoeffer. The second was to contain its propagation and further improvement, through most part of Europe, under the most celebrated printers; and the third an account of its introduction and progress into England. This, together with above one half of the first part, were happily finished, and produced by the time appointed, and met with more approbation and encouragement from his friends than I feared it would, being conscious how much better it might have turned out, would time have permitted it. And this I chiefly mention, not so much to excuse the defects of such a horrid performance, as because it hath given me since frequent occasion to observe how many much more considerable works have been spoiled, both at home and abroad, through the impatience of the subscribers; though this is far enough from being the only, or even the greatest inconvenience that attends most of those kinds of subscriptions.

As to Mr. Palmer, his circumstances were by this time so unaccountably low and unfortunate, considering the largeness and success of his business, and that he was himself a sober industrious man, and free from all extravagance, that he could not extricate himself by any other way, but by a statute of bankrupt, which caused his history to go sluggishly on; so that notwithstanding all the care and kind assistance of his good friend Dr. Mead, a stubborn distemper, which his misfortunes brought upon him, carried him off before the third part of it was finished. This defect, however, was happily supplied by the late noble earl of Pembroke, who being informed by Mr. Pain the engraver, Mr. Palmer's brother-in-law, what condition the remainder was left in, and that I was the person who had wrote the former parts, sent for me, and, with his usual generosity, enjoined me to compleat the work, according to the plan; and not only defrayed all the charges of it, even of the paper and printing, but furnished me with all necessary materials out of his own library; and, when the work was finished, his lordship reserved only some few copies to himself, and gave the remainder of the impression to Mr. Palmer's widow, not without some farther tokens of his liberality.

Before I leave this subject, I must, in justice to that noble peer, give an instance or two of his generosity and singular integrity. At my first coming into England, I had had the honour to be introduced to him, and to dine with him and other great persons in his company, and had received no small tokens of his regard, till he conceived a just disgust at one absurd fact I had affirmed in my fabulous history of Formosa, viz. the Greek tongue being taught there as a learned language, which monstrous absurdity sufficiently shewed my ignorance and indiscretion at the time of my writing it, and from that time his lordship gave me up for what I was, an impostor, and I saw him no more, till above twenty-eight years after, when Mr. Pine brought me to him, in order to finish the book abovementioned. At my first coming into his presence, his lordship presently knew me again, and reminded me of my having been often with him, and of the reason of his taking a dislike to me; upon which I readily owned the justness of the charge, and of his resentment, which I begged his lordship to look upon as the effect of a rash inconsiderate piece of youthful vanity, which I had long since disclaimed, and condemned myself for, and assured him, that I had since then, I thanked God, fallen into so laudable a way of living, as I doubted not his lordship, if he knew of it, would not but approve of. Mr. Pine confirmed what I had said; and his lordship with his usual affability and condescension, highly congratulated and commended me for it, and was pleased to express a more than ordinary pleasure at it, exhorting me to continue in the same good mind and way, and assuring me of his friendship and encouragement; and from that time I cannot sufficiently acknowledge his extreme benevolence and condescension, in not only furnishing me with all the books and other helps I wanted, but in his generously rewarding me for what I did; and when I was forced afterwards to acquaint him that I was a person concerned in the writing of the Universal History, became a subscriber and encourager of it, as I shall presently have occasion to shew. It was a little before Mr. Palmer's death, that this work, the project of which had been formed by Mr. Crockat, and the excellent plan by the late famed Mr. Sale, met with an unexpected stop, by an unhappy quarrel between the proprietors and the authors, at the head of whom was Mr. Sale abovementioned, when I was recommended to the former as a proper person to supply the place of some of the latter, who had absolutely declined being farther concerned in it. This rupture happened soon after the publication of the third number, anno

1730, when Mr. Palmer brought me the three printed numbers from the proprietors, and desired, if after having read them and the plan, I had a mind to engage myself in the work, I should give them and the rest of the authors a meeting at a place and day appointed, which I accordingly did, and after having informed myself with their terms, method, and other previous particulars, readily undertook to write the Jewish history, in which I was the most versed, and for which I knew myself already provided with a considerable quantity and variety of materials, which I had been collecting for my private use for several years; and as I have been one of the chief persons concerned as an author, not only in the first, but also in the second edition, and so was perfectly acquainted with every step taken in the progress of the work, the encouragements and difficulties it hath met with, as well as with the merit and demerit of every part of it, I shall make no difficulty to insert here a faithful and impartial account of the whole, at least so far as it may be of service to the public, and prove a means of making any future editions more compleat, by pointing out the many false steps which I found were impossible for us to avoid in the two former.

And here I must observe, in the first place, that though the design was publicly pretended to be carried on by a society of learned gentlemen, yet in fact Mr. Sale was to be the sole conductor of it, by the assistance of such ammanuenses as he should think fit to employ in the work. And though, in point of learning, no man might be better qualified than he, for such an arduous and extensive undertaking, yet his known strait circumstances obliged him to have so many other irons in the fire (to say nothing of his natural indolence, the sad effects of which, not only the proprietors of this work, but many others of that profession have sufficiently felt) that it was impossible for him to give it that attention which a work of that nature deserved, much less the dispatch he had engaged with them for, viz. the publishing twenty sheets per month. Accordingly upon enquiry I could not find that he ever wrote more than the first number; which, though puffed up with the specious pretence of a second edition, every reader versed on the subjects treated in it, might easily know where he had got all his materials ready gathered to his hand; yet so long was he in publishing it, that his delay occasioned the first misunderstanding between him and the proprietors, which was however followed by a greater.

The second and third numbers, which appeared afterwards to have been written by his two ammanuenses, till then unknown to the partners, came out indeed more regularly; but the proprietors, who had already paid Mr. Sale for them, were not a little surprised when the two young authors (whom I forbear naming, because they are both alive and make a good figure, the one in a high post, and the other in the commonwealth of learning) came and demanded the money for their copy. The propietors did indeed produce his receipts for much greater sums than the three numbers could amount to, but though they knew that he was not in a capacity to pay them, they refused to make a second disbursement for what they had more than payed for, whilst the sufferers, on the other hand, refused to go on further with the work, till they were satisfied for what they had done. The partners stiffly refusing to comply, the result was, that one of them not only quite declined all further meddling in the work, but vented his resentment by crying it down, and all the persons concerned in it, authors as well as proprietors. Mr. Sale was still more outrageous against them, of whom the latter had taken a note of 72 pounds, payable on demand, for money overpaid, and the embezzlement of a considerable number of books, which they had furnished him to carry on the design. This note was probably taken with a view of keeping him in awe, but neither that nor their threats could contain him within bounds, so that he became a most inveterate enemy to the design, and did all he could to discredit and obstruct it.

This was the hopeless situation of the work at my first being invited to it, and against which I cannot forbear mentioning another discouragement, viz. the freedom which the authors of the foregoing part had taken in reflecting, as often as they had opportunity, against the Mosaic account, especially in the history of the antient Canaanites, where God is recorded to have treated them with such severity in favour of the Israelites, and where they made no difficulty to reflect upon that partiality, as inconsistent with the divine justice and goodness towards a favourite nation, who are there represented as by far the worse of the two: for, as I took the liberty to observe to them, besides that all the objections against the divine conduct in this particular have been so often and so effectually answered by learned divines, that there can be no justifiable reason given for reviving them here, this manner of treating Moses's writings is far below the regard that such an antient and celebrated author may challenge, abstractedly even from his being acknowledged an inspired penman, by Jews, Turks and Christians. And therefore added, I will never engage in the work, unless you will allow me to follow the opposite tract, and, instead of reflecting, to vindicate both his character and writings, as often as occasion offers, either from the works of our best divines, or from sundry new observations I have had opportunity to make on the books of that divine lawgiver. I much question, if they had not been at such a nonplus for a hand to go immediately upon the Jewish history, whether they would have ever yielded to these terms, such was their opinion of Mr. Sale, whom they knew had no great regard for the Old Testament, and who had long ago inspired one, if not both of his ammanuenses with a most outrageous zeal against it. However, I got them with some trouble to acquiesce, and let me take my own way, only Mr. Provost, then one of the partners, begged it as a favour of me, that I would not be righteous over much.

I gave them soon after good cause to be satisfied with my advice and conduct, and the unexpected encouragement which the work met with, after the regular publication of two or three numbers of the Jewish history (to say nothing of the commendations given to it in print, by two such learned persons as Dr. Chapman, chaplain to his grace of Canterbury, and Dr. Pearce, rector of St. Martin's in the fields) raised it into such reputation and vogue, that they no longer doubted of its success; insomuch that they began now to enlarge the edition from 750 to 1000. And this I mention with pleasure, because the great call there was for it from that time, to what they had found before, when the numbers were returned to them by dozens from other booksellers, plainly shewed how few encouragers it would have met with among the freethinkers and unbelievers, to what it did among those of a different, and I may add, of a better way of thinking. There was indeed one main objection made, viz. my clashing with those who had gone before me; and I remember more particularly, that the late earl of Pembroke (who, as I lately hinted, was an encourager of the work, and to whom I was obliged to excuse my not waiting so often on him as he desired, in order to finish the third part of Mr. Palmer's history above mentioned, by acquainting his lordship that much of my time was taken up with the Universal History, in which I was engaged) expressed no small dislike at this contrast, or, as he was pleased to call it, chequer-work between the Jewish history, and some of the numbers that preceded it; the one expressing all along an unaccountable disregard for the Mosaic writings, whilst the other took all proper occasion to vindicate them, in a manner which he was pleased to call so very laudable and just; upon which I was forced to acquaint his lordship, that the former part had been printed some time before I was concerned in the work, and written by persons in a very different way of thinking from me, and which I had publicly disallowed; but as they had since declined the work, the proprietors had left me wholly at my liberty to take my own way, which I was fully determined to pursue to the end, so that there would be no more such contradictions to be found in the sequel, because all that related to the Jewish nation down to their dispersion at the destruction of Jerusalem, or even from that to the present time, if we were encouraged to continue it, would fall to my share; and that those who were to write the histories of the Assyrians, Medes, Persians, and other nations which had any connection with the Jewish, should be obliged to follow the same tract, and acknowledge the divine authority of the Old Testament. This his lordship highly approved, and as to the remaining difficulty, viz. the reconciling what was already printed, and he thought past remedying, I told his lordship, that the greatest part of these early numbers having been mislaid, and so bandied about and wasted that there would be speedily a necessity of reprinting them, I would engage to revise and correct them, so as to make the whole uniform, which was soon after done accordingly. But when, for the credit of the work, I proposed to the proprietors the calling in of the old numbers, and giving the purchasers the new ones in lieu of them, the greater part of them lent a deaf ear to it, alledging, that they were so much out of pocket already, that they could not afford to destroy so great a number of copies for the sake of uniformity, and that the work must take its chance without it.

This was not the only instance in which they stood in their own light; I shall beg leave to add one or two more. Before the ninth number of the first volume had been published, they had received several letters from the learned both at home and abroad, directed to the authors, particularly two from Holland, the one from a person who translated our history into French, and the other into Dutch, and published them there regularly every month, as we did here. These, among other commendations and encouragements, desired us to send them the sheets as fast as printed here, for the better dispatch of their version, and keeping time with us; offering to make any reasonable satisfaction for it, and to promote the credit and sale of the English original on the other side the water. The Dutch translator in particular, who was a man of learning and character, acquainted us, not without a handsome and modest apology, with some alterations and deviations he had taken the liberty to make from our printed copy, in the three or four first numbers, and desired us above all things to settle a correspondence with him, that we might freely communicate our thoughts to one another, promising to send us, at the conclusion of each volume a copy, of his version, with the alterations marked in the margin, and the sentiments of the learned beyond sea; about the work which he accordingly did at the close of his first volume, though we had not been able to prevail upon the proprietors to send them the sheets in the manner above desired, and were not willing to do it without their consent, they being all apprehensive that these would hinder the sale of the English original there. We tried in vain to convince them of the contrary, by shewing them that it would rather forward it, by making it more known and famed abroad; for that not only the English there, but likewise those who understood that language, would still chuse to read it in the original rather than in a version. I likewise tried to make them sensible how necessary and useful such a correspondence would be to us, and how much it would in all likelihood contribute to the credit and reputation of the work, and what need we stood in to use all proper helps, in a work of so arduous and extensive a nature. The only thing they would agree to, was that we might, if we thought fit, still correspond with them, (and that they knew we could do without their leave) but as to the sending the sheets as soon as printed, they absolutely refused; so that we were forced to put an end to the one for want of being able to comply with the other.

The next instance I shall give is still of a more sordid nature. They were obliged to furnish us with all necessary books for the work, and on my first going upon the Jewish history, I sent them a list of such as were really wanted, though some of them very considerable both in bulk and value, such as the Thalmuds, Polyglott, Opera Criticorum, &c. and was surprised at the difficulties they made, and objections they raised against both the number and charge of them, alledging on the one hand the vast number of them that had been formerly embezzled and lost, which they pretended to amount to near 200l. and on the other, the vast expence they had already been at, and the little returns made for it in the four first numbers; so that if I would not dispense with a good number of the dearest sort, they were afraid they must desist from proceeding farther. It was well for them, as well as me, that I had then a free access to Sion College library, by an order from the president and some of the heads of that society, and which I had made use of for some years, whenever I stood in need of it; so that I readily engaged to strike out all those that I should find there, provided they would promise to find me all the rest. By which means, as well as by the kind assistance of my good friend the reverend Mr. Reading, the late worthy library-keeper, who having the goodness to bring me all the books I called for, without the trouble of my looking out for them in their respective shelves, to my writing desk at the farther end of the library, I could with ease consult all my authors, make what extracts I wanted out of them, after which he took the pains of returning them to their proper places.

Now as this saved the booksellers the buying of near, if not more than 100l. worth of books, and me a great deal of trouble, (for Mr. Reading did most frequently enquire of me what part of a book I designed to consult, and being well acquainted with most of them, brought them to me opened at the very place I wanted, which enabled me to make more dispatch, and to keep up to the time of publication) I insisted at one of our meetings, and I thought justly too, that they should, by way of acknowledgement, present either the library, or the worthy keeper of it, with a set of volumes, as soon as they come out, which, I told them, might likewise be a means of recommending the work to those divines and others that frequented that place. They all seemed readily to agree to the proposal, and I acquainted Mr. Reading, who was not a little pleased with it, and told me, that, for his part, he was very ready to do all he could to promote our design, without any such view, though he said that he should be glad to see it presented to the library, as it was a work which he much approved as far as we had gone, the chronology excepted, to which he thought that of the learned Usher vastly preferable. I told him I was wholly of his opinion, and was sorry Mr. Sale had ever fixed upon this, but that it was done before I was concerned in the work, and could not now be retrieved, at least in this first edition, but by the readers making up the difference either in their mind or with the pen. I added, that I had reason to believe, that if the work came ever to be reprinted, we should exchange it for that of Archbishop Usher, as we have actually done. However, as soon as the first part of the Jewish history was printed off, I took a little recess among some of my friends in Hampshire, where I compleated my next task, viz. the history of the Celtes and the Scythians, and as I had the free use of several libraries there, I saved the proprietors the charge of buying those books I was sure to find in any of them, and as soon as I found by the public papers, that the first volume was published, wrote a letter to put them in mind of their promise of presenting one of them to Sion College library; but I was much surprised at my coming to town, to find that they had absolutely resolved against it, on pretence that it might hinder many clergymen from buying it, if they could have the reading of it there. I tried in vain to forewarn them that I should want most of the same scarce and chargeable books, besides a number of others, for the writing the second part of the Jewish history, in a subsequent volume, in which case they could not expect that I should again have recourse to my good friend Mr. Reading, but must of necessity be at the expence of buying them; they chose to run the hazard of it, and I took care not to spare them in one of them, when it came to the point.

From these few instances, the reader may easily guess that the then partners were not quite so solicitous for the credit of the work, as might have been wished, considering how well it took by this time. But I must in justice to them acquaint him, that (besides the great difficulties they laboured under to procure proper hands to go on with it, and for which I refer him to what I have said in the dedication and preface to the last volume of the folio edition) they had met with many unexpected and considerable losses; some of the newly engaged authors, for instance took up pretty round sums before-hand, and never wrote a line of the part they had undertaken; others, even among the old ones, wrote theirs in such a careless manner as not to be fit to appear in print, when they came to be examined by the rest, and yet were paid the same to the full as if their copy had passed muster, though the whole was to be done again de novo, and the retarding of the work was an additional loss to the proprietors. I will add, that I have since known near twenty sheets of the beginning of the Byzantine history, done by a judicious hand, and printed off, yet condemned to waste paper chiefly because it was spun to too great a length, which was still a much greater loss. The truth is, that the author of the Roman history, having wire-drawn it to above three times the length it was to have been, there was an absolute necessity of curtailing that of the Constantinopolitan emperors, to prevent the work swelling into an enormous bulk; and he himself hath abridged it in such a manner as hath quite marred it, since the reader will find most reigns contained in as many short paragraphs as they would have required sheets, which is so much the greater loss to the public, inasmuch as the Roman history being so well known, and written by so many hands, was the fittest to have been thus epitomised; whereas the Byzantine, though equally curious and instructive, is so little known, that it ought to have been written in a more copious manner, especially as it abounds with the most interesting incidents to the church as well as the state. So that the author hath done in both respects the very reverse of what he ought to have done.

The reader may, from the instances above mentioned, suppose perhaps, that we the authors kept constantly to our meetings and examining each part in a body, as we used to do at first setting out, a method of the greatest consequence towards the carrying on such a work, and which the proprietors were not wanting in generosity to promote; but we soon found the new comers so averse to continue it, or submit the review of their copy to the old ones, that they either absented themselves from our meetings, or else condescended only to answer such questions as were asked them by the old ones concerning their fixing any point of history, which had a connection with that of another nation; as the Macedonians and Greeks, for instance, done by two or three hands, to prevent our clashing with each other about uncertain or controverted facts; in every respect, they insisted on going on each in his own way, as they were, they told us, sufficiently acquainted with the subject they had in hand. By this means it was that they indulged themselves in the liberty of going beyond their bounds, and swelling each part to double the bulk agreed on, by often repeating the same common facts in each separate history, which we had agreed should be related at length but in its proper place, whilst every other occasion that offered for fresh mention of them, was to be only referred to that, either as promiscua to follow in the sequel, or as a reference to what hath already been said.

For we had from the beginning agreed upon this method, that nothing should be related at length concerning the history of any nation or country, but what was transacted within the boundaries of it; and that the wars, conquests, &c. which were carried on abroad, should be mentioned chiefly in the history of those countries where they were made; to do otherwise, would be, as was hinted at the beginning of the first volume, treating those conquered nations with the same arbitrary contempt and neglect as their conquerors had formerly done. Thus, for instance, it was resolved that Alexander's history should be confined to Macedonia, and his other conquests referred to that of those nations he subdued; that that of the Romans, should be confined within the limits of Italy, and their new lawless acquisitions referred to the history of the Gauls, Germans, Spaniards, Carthaginians, &c. that were to follow. This would at once have effectually cut off all needless repetitions, with which the work hath been swelled beyond its designed length, without docking the history of any nation, as we have been since forced to do, to avoid falling into the same fault in which the writers of the several Greek histories have fallen, where the reader may see the same facts related over and over in the histories of the

Macedonians, Athenians, Spartans, &c. not without some visible and unjustifiable variations, all which might easily have been avoided, had the authors kept within the rules abovementioned. But no one hath shewn a greater disregard to them, than the author of the Roman history, who hath swallowed up all the unhappy nations that fell into those conquerors clutches without distinction, and expatiated with the same diffuseness on their history without, as he hath in that within their territories, which though some of our readers have approved of, as it gives a more connected history of that nation, a thing so much the less needful in a work of this extensive nature, as we have it written in a body by so many different hands, yet hath been highly disliked by the far greater, and I may add the more judicious part of them, as contrary to our plan and engagements to the public, and to the nature of an Universal History, wherein that of every nation, should be found fully displayed, and every fact confined to its proper scene of action. It was to the neglect of attending to, or rather keeping up to this original design, that we must ascribe two considerable defects in the work, against which our readers have justly complained. The one, that some histories, as for instance, that of the Carthaginians, had been fraught with an unnecessary repetition of all their wars with the Romans, or which had been already fully related in the Roman history, to the swelling of the work beyond its due limits; the other, that to avoid that inconveniency and charge to the purchasers, those of the Gauls, Germans and Spaniards are truncated, and their wars with, and reduction by the Romans are barely referred to what hath been said in the Roman history, where they are scattered and so interspersed with that of other nations, that it cannot be called a regular and compleat history of them. And what is this but absorbing all these brave nations by the lump, into that of their tyrannic conquerors; and how could I, to whose lot the history of those three ancient nations fell, avoid it by any other way, but that of recapitulating all afresh, in the most compendious manner I could, to avoid swelling the work and referring the reader to the volume and page of the Roman history, where the facts are mentioned at length. And there was by that time the more cause to abridge all these needless repetitions, because the purchasers, and after them the booksellers, had justly complained, how vastly the work was already swelled beyond the bounds to which we had promised to confine it. But this was not so readily complied with by the rest, who having finished each their respective histories, according to the plan and method agreed upon, and mentioned above, and either did not dream that the writer of the Roman history would go contrary, or when they found he had, did resent it too much to suffer their own to be truncated on his account, insisted upon their being printed at full length, and with all their repetitions. And this the booksellers were forced to submit to, for fear not only of disobliging the authors, but likewise of retarding the regular publication of the volumes.

But what will easily convince the reader, as it hath me long since, how much more earnest the writer of the Roman history was to promote his own ignoble interest, at the expence of the proprietors as well as the credit of the work, is, that when he came afterwards to write the second part of the history of the Persians, he hath repeated at length all their wars with the eastern emperors, together with all the other facts and incidents that passed between them, at full length, instead of referring to what he had formerly said in the Byzantine history; for this plainly shews that the dulcis odor lucri, more effectually influenced him than all the complaints of the proprietors and purchasers, which last were become so rife that we thought it necessary to publish something by way of excuse for this excess of bulk, and at the same time to make the best appology we could for that and other deviations from our original plan, without discovering the causes they were owing to, which would have rather helped to discredit the work in the eye of the world, which did not dream how little unanimity there was in our proceedings, and how impossible it was for the best inclined of us to keep such selfish spirits as were then employed, within the bounds prescribed. I shall now give a farther instance of it, and such a pregnant one, as will convince the reader that such a work as this could never be carried on fairly, and according to our promise, notwithstanding all our care and precaution, even in the second impression of the work; how much less possible must it have been, to have done so in the first.

But there was still a greater inconvenience resulting from these repetitions, and the monstrous bulk of the Roman history, and by that time the seventh volume was finished, the public began to think we designed to spin the work to nine or ten, for there were still a great number of ancient kingdoms and countries to be described, according to our original design, such as the Mohammedan history, and other nations interwoven with it, consisting of above twenty articles in Mr. Sale's plan, most of them of such hard names as few readers were acquainted with, besides the kingdoms of the great Mogul and other parts of India, those of Siam, China, Japan, Tartary, Russia both in Europe and Asia, the Turkish empire in both, and the whole country of America; all which could hardly be contained in less than two volumes at the least. However, by that time the seventh volume was published, the proprietors met with so little encouragement to go on from the purchasers, and were already such considerable losers, that they thought fit to stop there, and leave the work thus maimed and imperfect; but what not only determined, but in some measure forced them to it, was their having the mortification soon after, to see their property invaded by three different pyratical booksellers of Dublin, who, as they were not at any other charge than printing and paper, both which are much cheaper in Ireland than here, could well enough afford it to the public for half the price that ours sold for at London, and unknown to each other reprinted the work there word for word, two of them in folio and the third in octavo, and when each of them came to understand that the like pyracy had been committed by the other two, fell foul against each other in their advertisements, in such language and opprobrious names as all three justly deserved. As therefore such a piece of flagrant injustice could not but greatly affect the original proprietors, who were already so considerably losers, it could not be expected that they should run the manifest hazard of throwing away more money in pursuit of their plan. We were therefore obliged to frame another kind of excuse for their dropping it, viz. that those countries and kingdoms not spoken of in the foregoing volumes, being of later discovery, such as India, China, &c. in Asia, a great part of Africa, and the new American world, they would be more properly described, and their histories begun and continued in the modern part, which they were however no farther resolved to go on with, than as they found a probability of its meeting more encouragement than the old had hitherto done. So that they had now time to think on some proper means of suppressing the three pyrated impressions as far as possible, by exposing them to the public as they justly deserved, and proposing to give the world a new and more correct edition of the whole in octavo, together with additions of such material points as had been omitted in the former.

When this second impression came to be resolved on, both the authors and proprietors, sensible of the many miscarriages of the former, for want of our following our first plan, did unanimously agree among other things, that every one of us in the revising, correcting, and improving each our respective parts, should oblige ourselves, so far to stick close to it for the future, that all the unnecessary repetitions should be rescinded, and every historical fact be confined to the history of that country in which it was transacted, and no where mentioned at length but there; as the conquest of Sicily in the history of that Island, of Carthage in that of the Republic, of the Spaniards, Gauls, &c. in that of those nations, which was the only way of making every one of them compleat, and at the same time shorten the work, by the avoiding all needless repetitions. And this we not only promised, but bound ourselves in writing to perform; however to make the point still more sure, as I had reason to doubt an unanimous compliance to the agreement from one quarter, I further proposed that no part should go to the press, till it had been examined and approved by the rest. This was accordingly opposed by the party I suspected under several specious pretences, such as taking up too much time, as we lived at some distance from each other, the danger of mislaying or losing some of the copy, and having now and then some alteration in controverted points, all which might retard if not hinder the work; upon which the proprietors thought fit to give it up, and to depend upon our honour for the exact performance of our agreement. However, as he hath hardly in one single instance kept up to it, but hath reprinted, not only his own Roman history, but several other parts done formerly by other hands, and now committed to his care by the booksellers, almost verbatim from the first edition, to the no small trouble of, and damage to the other authors who had filled up these unnecessary chasms in their respective parts, which he should have struck out of his own, and have been since obliged to erase all those additions; he hath sufficiently convinced every one of us what his views were in so strenuously opposing my proposal, and consequently how impossible it is for such a design as this to be rightly executed, unless the whole care and revisal be left to one single person of ability equal to it. The thing is now past all remedy with respect to this second edition, though it may be easily rectified in every respect in a future one, if any such may ever find encouragement. But the wrong done to the public in this second, is the more considerable, through the unfairness of the author above mentioned, in as much as, though he is the only one concerned, that hath not complied with our articles, he has by his subdulous artifice had the far greater share in the work committed to him. And I think I have the greater right to complain of his breach of promise, and the discredit he hath brought on us and the work, as I can make it appear that neither in the first nor second edition, I have ever departed from our original plan, in any of those parts I have been engaged in, nor inserted any thing in them except by way of promissum or reference, that properly belonged to another. And for the truth of this I shall only appeal to these parts, a list of which I shall, in justice to my own character, now give to the reader.

1. The Jewish history, from Abraham, to the Babylonish captivity.
2. The history of the Celtes and Scythians.
3. The ancient history of Greece, or the fabulous and heroic times.
4. The sequel of the Jewish history, from the return from Babylon, to the destruction of Jerusalem by Titus.
5. The history of the ancient Empires of Nice and Trebizon.
6. The history of the ancient Spaniards.
7. Of the Gauls.
8. Of the ancient Germans.

In the second edition, wherein we endeavoured to supply all the material omissions in the first, the following parts came to my share, viz.

The sequel of the Theban, and Corinthian history.

1. The Retreat of Xenophon.

2. The continuation of the Jewish history, from the destruction of Jerusalem by Titus, to this present time.

I must here observe with respect to the last of these, that it had been promised in our plan from the very beginning, but had been deferred, as more properly belonging to the modern history; upon which several of our subscribers and correspondents complained of the omission, as it is a subject not only curious and instructive, but likewise little known, and therefore much wanted; upon which we had agreed to satisfy their demand, and to have inserted it at the end of the second part of the Jewish or the Roman history, and I had accordingly prepared it for the press against that time, and bestowed full six months in the writing of it, besides what I had spent before in collecting such curious materials as fell in my way; so that the copy, which will make about fifteen or sixteen sheets of the octavo edition, hath been a good while in the hands of the proprietors, and as I had reason to expect, would have been printed before now in the fifteenth or sixteenth volume, of which I had apprised several of my correspondents, as well as those of my acquaintance who enquired after it. But to my surprise, the proprietors have since determined to postpone it till the Modern History comes out, as it brings the history of the Jewish nation down to the present time, which no other in the work doth, and can have no place in the Antient. But the real cause was the want of room, the work being like to swell beyond the number of volumes promised in their proposals.

The truth is they being in some measure obliged to include it within the compass of twenty, or at most twenty-one volumes, in order to suppress the pyratical Irish edition (which was promised to be contained within that number, though without any probability (or perhaps design) of their so doing, if one may guess by the bulk of each of those volumes that have been published) there was a necessity of reducing matters within a narrower compass. And this upon a strict computation might have been easily done, notwithstanding the several additions that were to be made to the work, had all the needless repetitions been rescinded, the style made more concise, and a great number of superfluous facts, circumstances, disquisitions, and controversies, most of them useless and incompatible with the nature of so extensive a work, been struck out of both the text and notes, as we had agreed should be done by every one in his respective parts, and hath been actually done by all but one, and him the person who had the largest share in the revising and contracting of the work; so that through his neglect and noncompliance, the work hath swelled not only much beyond our computation, but would have done much more so, had not the proprietors from a laudable desire of keeping up as much as could possibly be done to the first proposals, not only generously thrown in five or six sheets extraordinary into every volume, but likewise enlarged every page both in the length and number of the lines, by which each volume from the fourth downwards, may be justly said to contain between six or seven sheets more of matter than was originally proposed, or than the third or fourth contained. And this I am bound to mention in justice to them, because though they were considerable losers by the first edition, they yet chose to put themselves to this extraordinary expence, rather than incur the charge of imposing upon the public, by the unexpected addition of three or four volumes more than they had engaged to comprise the whole work in. However, I cannot but be sorry that these considerations should be looked upon as a sufficinet pretext for their suppressing that sequel of the Jewish history I have been speaking of, contrary to the original plan of the work, and the expectation of so many of its encouragers. And I do purposely take notice of it, that in case I can not prevail upon them to print it at the end of the work, and leave it at the option of subscribers, either to buy or leave it, the public may know where the fault lies, and that my friends may not lay it at my door.

Thus much may suffice for the history of this work, and to account for the great imperfections of the first edition, and for the second not turning out better than it hath; and I doubt not, when the reader considers all these things he will be apt rather to wonder, as I have often done, that it is come out so well as it is. I have no intention, much less any cause to reflect on the proprietors of the work, especially those who are become so since the deaths or failure of most of the old ones. They have spared neither pains nor cost towards its improvement, nor been wanting in generosity to the authors. They never once disputed with me about the price I set upon my labour, nor refused to supply me with such sums as I drew upon them for. This is indeed more than I can or ought to say of the old set of them, some of whom often put us to great difficulties by their sordidness and mutual jealousies and misunderstandings, all which I with pleasure observed to vanish upon the coming in of this new set. It is true that as far as related to me, they always found me diligent and punctual; I performed the parts I undertook to the best of my ability, and being content with a moderate gain, could bestow the more time and labour upon them, and always took care to have them finished at the time required; and so wholly, and I may add cordially, was I intent upon the work in general, that I would never engage in any other whilst that lasted. And this they were so far satisfied of, and so entirely relied on me, that whether in town or country, I have been allowed to drawn upon Mr. Millar, for some scores of pounds before hand, which were punctually answered by him, though neither he nor any of the partners, ever saw any of my copy till it went to the press; and when printed off paid the surplus with uncommon generosity, for I always took care to keep within compass. This may look like vanity for me to say of myself, but as it will not be made public till after my death, when I shall be out of the way of reaping any satifaction from it, but the consciousness of having acted an honest part; and as this hath been my constant method with all the booksellers with whom I have been concerned, and for this I dare appeal to all who have employed me, I am the less scrupulous about any sinister construction a censorious reader may put upon it; those who have known me and my conversation for much above these twenty years, will I hope pass a more candid judgment upon it.

However, with respect to the management of the partners about this second edition, I cannot but observe that they were guilty of two fatal errors. The first in committing so great a share of the work, as well as the revisal of the whole to a man, who they had all reason to believe aimed chiefly at gain and dispatch, and to agree with him by the lump as they did, which would only prove a temptation to him to hurry it off as fast as he could, and as he accordingly did, to their no small mortification, as well as hurt to themselves and the work. I might add, that as he was and owned himself quite unacquainted with the eastern languages, he was the most unqualified for several parts that fell to his lot of any and if care had not been taken would have committed such mistakes in the very spelling of proper names, as would quite have discredited it.

The other was their engaging to publish a volume monthly, and beginning to publish before they had a sufficient number ready printed before hand, to have enabled them to keep up to their time; the want of which precaution hath since obliged them to have several volumes on the anvill at different presses at once, and to be dispatched with such precipitation that the compositors have overlooked many litteral errors which had been corrected by the authors, and which is still worse, this hath likewise made it impossible for us to make the proper and necessary references from one volume to the other as they were printed at the same time, and not regularly one after another, as they should have done, so that in some cases we could hardly refer to the volume much less to the page; but the reader will find many instances of this last.

I shall now give some few useful hints how this work may be made compleat in a future edition by one single hand, if equal to the task; first, let whoever undertakes it read it all over again attentively and regularly, one volume after another, and as he reads, common-place every thing, person, fact, &c. as if he designed it for a compleat and copious index. Let him not depend upon that general one which is ready made to his hand, at the end of the work, and where all these needless repetitions, inconsistences, and contradictions may be artfully omitted or concealed, but either make a full and exact one de novo, or at least consult the printed one upon every point he reads over, and mark down every such omission or concealment; though were it my case I should rather prefer the former, because there will be the less labour lost, as it will stand ready for such when the work comes to be reprinted, and he will have afterwards nothing to do but add the printed pages to every article as they come in course, only if it should be deemed too full, he may strike out afterwards such as appear of less moment. But he will find this singular benefit by such an exact common-placing of every thing, that it will discover to him at once every needless repetition, every inconsistency and contradiction as he reads on, which he may at the same time mark down in the margin of the book, in order to correct them on the second reading. He may then set down likewise in the margin, the volume and page where the same thing is told before, where it is differently related or set in a different light, and in cases that admit a dispute, by consulting the original authors, be able to judge which is right or most probable. Thus for instance, when he finds the very same facts related in the histories of Sicily, Rome and Carthage, he will easily know where they ought to have been set down at length, namely, where the scene of action happened, and where only to be referred to it, viz. in the other two. So that whatever either the Romans or Carthaginians transacted in Sicily, should be only promised or referred to in their history, and only related at full length in that of the Sicilians; and so of the rest. He will likewise by such an index find out where any facts or transactions have been differently related or represented by each of their writers, who must of course be supposed, and will upon trial be found to clash often, for want of frequently conferring with each other, or duly consulting and examining, or perhaps some times of rightly understanding the original authors they pretend to follow.

By this means he will likewise be able to discover many facts related in one place, which more properly belong to, or might be more conveniently transferred to another, and place them so accordingly in his marginal notes. By that time he hath common-placed the whole set of volumes, he will be likewise able to discover every material omission under every article, either from his own memory and reading, or by turning to the index of such books as treat of the same subject, and be able to supply every such defect from them. Thus in the articles of nations, as Jews, Egyptians, Romans, &c. or of cities, as Jerusalem, Alexandria, Rome, &c. if he finds any thing material, which not being in his common-place book, makes him conclude it was omitted in the work, he will likewise easily supply from those authors and their indexes, and the same may be done by the articles of names of kingdoms, provinces, monarchs, &c. by furnishing himself with the best modern authors who have wrote of them, and supplying each with every thing he finds wanting in his own common-place book, as well as exchange some less material trifles that are in this, for more momentous ones he will find in them, all which may be done with little trouble, and he will still reserve to himself the liberty of the difference in controverted points he will meet with among those moderns, by having recouse to the original ones; for he must make it a standing rule to himself, not to rely on the former which are more copious than exact, without consulting the latter, and where those differ among themselves as they often do, to use all proper helps either to reconcile them, or to chuse the more probable side.

This would have been the method I should have taken, had I had any share in the revising any other but my own particular parts in the work; tho' I must still have thought it too much for any one to have revised the whole, and should have thought it necessary to have imparted the above mentioned rules to the rest, in order to have enabled them to have rectified every mistake, contrast, and jarring, between their parts. For as I knew that all the hopes of the proprietors, was in a second, and more correct edition, to reimburse the losses they had sustained by the first; I had their consent to compose the index to each of the volumes, (the first excepted, which was done by the same hand that wrote the Roman history, and justly condemned for its unnecessary length and verbosity) by which I could observe as I read along, and marked in the margin of the leaves, every needless repetition, superfluity, contrariety, omission, transposition, &c. that would be necessary to make the next impression more compleat, especially when I came to make the general one to the whole; and was the better inabled by it, to rescind and alter what I found amiss or superfluous in those parts that came more immediately under my care, though I have had since reason to think I have gone too far in it, and out of complaisance to the proprietors, who complained that my Jewish history was too diffuse for a work of this nature, have been prevailed on to strike out in this second edition many curious things, which I have since found had been very well liked and approved of in the first. But without such rescisions it was imposble to bring the whole within the compass proposed, especially as they were so much neglected in several other parts of the work, which would at least as conveniently admit of them, such as the Dynastes of the Egyptians, the history of Persia from the oriental writers, and many other such fabulous absurdities. However, I cannot accuse myself of having suppressed any thing that was of moment in that history; though several perhaps, and to my no small regret, which would have been acceptable to the curious in that kind of learning. As for all the other parts within my province, I have rather enlarged and improved them with new proofs, observations and curious additions, as may be easily found by comparing the two editions together.

With relation to the desiderata in both editions, I cannot forbear taking notice that the ancient history of the northern nations, such as Moscovy, Poland, Sweden, Denmark, Norway, &c. hath been altogether omitted except some few hints that have been given in that of the Scythians and Celtes, intimating only that the former were originally descended from the latter. It is indeed commonly believed that these remote nations have no records of their ancient times, but I had a singular opportunity of being convinced of the contrary, by a learned gentleman who was a professor of history, &c. in the university of Abbo in Norway, but came to London mostly every summer as an agent from the king of Sweden, and among other new books, used to buy several setts of the Universal History for that Prince, for count Coningsegg, and other great persons in that kingdom. This gentleman having expressed a desire to Mr. Symons his bookseller, and one of the proprietors, of conversing with one of the authors, particularly with that of the Jewish history, we soon came acquainted together, and upon my enquiring of him after such records or monuments of those northern nations on which one might compile their ancient history, gave me such a satisfactory account, as made me persuade Mr. Symon, and the other partners, to engage him to undertake it, which he, with some difficulty, agreed to do, notwithstanding his other avocations. I had the pleasure of seeing him every time he came to London, and to hear how well he proceeded in the work; and accordingly in about three years he brought a large and elaborate account of all the northern nations and countries, their origin, ancient settlements, history, &c. with many curious observations on their geography, natural history, and the whole backed with such good authorities and proofs, as one would hardly have expected from such barren climes, and was recommended by several of the most learned men in Sweden and Norway, who had the perusal, or even contributed to some part or other of it.

This chapter, which, according to our original plan, was to have preceded the irruption of the Huns, Goths, Vandals, Suevi and into the southern parts of Europe, would have given a much better and clearer account of these barbarous nations, than that which hath been given in the history of their new settlements in Hungary, Italy, France, Spain, &c. The misfortune was, that it proved too bulky (though nothing could be said to be superfluous or impertinent in it) it being computed to amount to above seventy folio sheets, for which they could not find room, our work being already swolen vastly beyond its bulk; so that Dr. Sidenius, that was the learned author's name, had the mortification of having that curious part refused by the proprietors, and returned upon his hands, the old ones, as Mess. Symon and Batley, being dead, and the rest, except Mr. Osborne in Grays-Inn, being gone off, and the new ones not looking upon themselves concerned in the agreement. And this I mention with no small regret, because it was a considerable loss to the learned world, as well as to the author, and such as I much fear will hardly be ever recovered.

In the interval between the conclusion of the first, and the resolution of printing the second, I was invited into a share of the new System of Geography, in which though the Public found just fault with the extravagant length of that which related to Great Britain and Ireland, I yet found the authors concerned in it, so well qualified for the work, so communicative and punctual in their regular meetings once a fortnight, that I readily came into it, and found with pleasure the work carried on with more unanimity, exactness, and to the satisfaction of the proprietors, as well as of the public. The parts I did in that work were those that follow. 1. Spain, Portugal and the islands belonging to them. 2. Italy, Savoy, Piedmont, and the islands of Sicily, Sardinia, Corsica, &c. 3. Muscovy both in Europe and Asia. 4. Turky in Asia. 5. In Asia, China, Japan, Jetzo, and the islands along those coasts, particularly that of Formosa, which part I chose, that I might take occasion publickly to acknowledge, as it were by a third hand, the falshood and imposture of my former account of that island. 6. In Africa, the kingdoms of Egypt, Abyssinia, Lybia, Barbary, Tripoli, Tunis, Morocco, Fez, with an account of the Mediterranean Sea, and the famed river of Sanaga. 7. The Azores islands. 8. In America, the countries of Brasil, Magellan, Terra del Fuego, Canada, Louisiana, and the Bahamas and Bermudas islands. And by the time I had concluded these last, I was called upon to prepare my respective parts of the Universal History, for the second impression mentioned above. I have however found sufficient reason to complain of the wrong management of this work in several respects, though otherwise carried on with greater exactness and unanimity than that of the Universal History, and I shall now take the liberty of mentioning some of the most considerable ones, because they have been the cause of some unavoidable errors and blunders, not only in the two above mentioned works, but in most others that have been published in the same or near the same way. The first is the authors being tied to produce such a number of sheets in so short a time as is almost incompatible with their desire, if any such they have, of performing their respective parts with any exactness; for, though the publishers seldom fail of acquainting the public that the work is either already, or pretty near finished and ready for the press, so that there is no danger of its meeting with any delay or impediment, yet that is seldom if ever the case, and with respect to the works I am speaking of, I found it quite the reverse, and that they have frequently been sent to the press, under the promise of being regularly published, by such a number of sheets every week or month, when scarcely a fourth part of it was written. So that, to prevent the retarding of the work, they have been obliged to call in for new helps, whom they have obliged to engage to perform their part in less than half the time, that it would have reasonably required; considering that they not only had it all to begin and go through in that short space, as was the case in this new System of Geography, but that some of them were likewise engaged in some other work, between which and this, they were forced to divide their time and diligence, though either of them did more than require it all; and how could it be possible for either to be performed as it ought?

Another mismanagement from the beginning was, the interlarding every fourth or fifth number with a set of maps which indeed gave some breathing time to the authors, but then it confined them to receive all their directions concerning the limits, situation, longitude, latitude, distances, &c. from those maps, which being such as the engraver rather than the authors had made choice of, as the most authentic in his opinion, were not always so judiciously chosen as could have been wished. This made many errors remediless and irretrievable, because the greatest part of those maps had been published in such numbers, several months before the authors were called upon to begin the geography of those countries. This I often complained of to the proprietors from the beginning, both as a great oversight and a hardship upon the authors, who, instead of being allowed to direct the engraver in the choice or compiling of them, were obliged to follow him implicitly, and often contrary to their own opinion and liking, in those which he had thought fit to pitch upon for our guide. Thus in the map of Japan, for instance, the land of Jetzo is affirmed to be the same with Cumschatta, though contrary to fact, it not being so much as part of it. I might add likewise, that those maps confined us to the orthography of places, though very often erroneous, or being of foreign extract, conveyed a wrong sound of the name to an English ear.

But the most considerable mismanagement was in the choice of such printers as bore indeed the greatest sway and interest, and who consequently had such a glut of business, that every thing was dispatched with the utmost hurry and precipitation, in order to keep up to their time. This never failed causing a great deal of confusion and incorrectness in the printing, particularly in the othography of proper names, and giving the authors a great deal of trouble in correcting the proofs, which, however, was but too often of no service, through the hurry the compositors were in, which made them overlook and often neglect those corrections. It frequently happened likewise, that they required such a quick dispatch of the author, in correcting the sheets, that they had not time enough to read them over with that carefulness they would otherwise have done; so that they themselves could not avoid overlooking even some material errors in the spelling, but most chiefly in the numbers and figures. As for me, it being my constant rule not to be engaged in two works at once, I never would let a proof go out of my hands, without a second, and, in some cases, a third reading, but I have often found that I might as well have saved myself that labour, since the correctors or compositors had not time enough left to make the proper emendations, and sometimes have sent the sheet to the press before the proof hath been returned.

To prevent this unfair dealing, as I may justly call it, or at least to lay the blame at the right door, I had taken a method of insisting upon having two proofs, of each sheet, sent me from the press; under pretence of keeping one of them by me, to refer to when it was requisite, but in fact by correcting both proofs alike in the margin, to be able to produce that which I kept by me, against both the compositor, and corrector, when ever they were guilty of any such neglect. But as soon as my design was found out by them, some plausible excuses were made, for not continuing to send duplicates, and I was forced to give up that point, unless I had a mind to disoblige the very master printers, who were some of the richest, and bore the greatest sway with the proprietors, and had already deprived us, under the pretence of dispatch, of the privelege of revising our copy, after our first correction. This last indeed was denied us, on account of the unreasonable trouble, which one of the authors too frequently gave them, in those revises at the first setting out? who did often require three or four of them, and every one loaded with new, and mostly needless alterations, which took up so much of the compositors time that they were obliged to complain of it. This was, though true with respect to one author, but a poor pretence for depriving the rest of the liberty of one single revise, which they chiefly insisted on, not so much to make any necessary alterations, as only to be satisfied that none of their corrections were overlooked. However, the point was overruled by the printers; and that material check being taken off from the compositors, the literal errors multiplied so fast upon us, especially in the words and quotations out of the eastern languages, that we were obliged to take notice only of such as were of the greatest moment in the table of errata of the first edition, and to curtail as many of those foreign words as we could in the second, especially those of the Arabic, Hebrew, and Syriac kind.

These are some of the principal causes of that incorrectness which commonly, I had almost said unavoidably, happen in these kinds of works, let an author be ever so desirous and careful to avoid them, unless he hath so great a sway over the printers, that they dare not refuse him the liberty of revising his own work as often as he sees it needful. And the least that he can insist on, for his own credit and satisfaction, is a revisal of every proof after it hath been corrected by him.

I did take occasion to mention a little higher the wrong information which Mr. Palmer gave me concerning Bishop Hare's Metrical Psalter, which was, unknown to me, put into Mr. Bowyer's hands to print, whilst I was writing the first part of the Jewish history, and as there had elapsed several years between the time, in which Mr. Palmer was applied to by Dr. Washburn, and that of my becoming in course to write on the subject of the Hebrew poetry, which had confirmed me in the opinion that the bishop's design was quite set aside; I made no difficulty to affirm after the generality of the learned writers on that subject, that the metre of the Hebrew Psalms and other poetical pieces in the Old Testament, was looked upon as irretrievably lost, notwithstanding the efforts of some, and the pretences of others, who vainly imagined they had or were in the way of recovering it. I backed my opinion with some new arguments which had occurred to me during my fruitless search after it, and which appeared to me to carry no small force. This part, which was contained in the ninth number of the first volume, was scarcely published, before the bishop's Psalter came out. It may be easily imagined that my curiosity would not permit me to be long without examining that performance, which seemed to overthrow all that I had said on that subject, and sadly was I vexed that my part was published before I had seen this unexpected piece. Had I dreamed of any such being so near coming out, I would doubtless have suppressed mine till I had thereby examined it. What surprised me most, and made me entertain some higher notion of that enterprize, was the long interval which had passed between the time of its being finished and offered to Mr. Palmer, and that of its being published, which I reckon to have been about six or seven years, and which I therefore supposed the bishop and his learned friend Dr. W — —, had spent in the revising and polishing it; but, upon stricter enquiry, I found the cause of that delay to have been of a different nature, and was as follows.

His lordship had excepted against Mr. Palmer's Hebrew types, which were of Athias's font, and a little battered, and insisted upon his having a new sett from Mr. Caslon, which greatly exceeded it in beauty. But Mr. Palmer was so deep in debt to him, that he knew not well how to procure it from him without ready money, which he was not able to spare. The bishop likewise insisted upon having some Roman and Italic types cast with some distinguishing mark, to direct his readers to the Hebrew letters they were designed to answer, and these required a new sett of punches and matrices before they could be cast, and that would have delayed the work, which Mr. Palmer was in haste to go about, that he might the sooner finger some of his lordship's money. This put him upon such an unfair stratagem, which when discovered, quite disgusted his lordship against him, viz. representing Mr. Caslon as an idle, dilatory workman, who would in all probability make them wait several years for those few types, if ever he finished them. That he was indeed the only artist that could supply him with those types, but that he hated work, and was not to be depended upon, and therefore advised his lordship to make shift with some sort which he could substitute; and would answer the same purpose, rather than run the risk of staying so long, and being perhaps disappointed. The bishop, however, being resolved, if possible, to have the desired types, sent for Mr. Bowyer, and asked him whether he knew a letter founder that could cast him such a sett out of hand, who immediately recommended Mr. Caslon; and, being told what a sad and disadvantageous character he had heard of him, Mr. Bowyer not only assured his lordship that it was a very false and unjust one, and engaged to get the above-mentioned types cast by him, and a new font of his Hebrew ones, in as short a time as the thing could possibly be done. Mr. Caslon was accordingly sent for by his lordship, and having made him sensible of the time the new ones would require to be made ready for use, did produce them according to his promise, and the book was soon after put to the press; and this it was that had so long retarded its publication.

I was not long without it, and must own that his preface, in which his lordship confuted, with uncommon learning and keeness, all the systems that hitherto appeared in public, raised my expectation to a high degree. For if the metre of the sacred book could but be supposed to come up to the loftiness and dignity of the thoughts and expressions, (and who could ever have doubted of it, that considers how much greater genius the latter requires than the former?) it must I thought have greatly excelled that of Homer and Virgil. But how great was my surprise, when upon reading on I found that his lordship had reduced it to a poor low, crawling humdrum, bitony of trochaics and iambics, or vice versa as the reader pleased, and into which he might with ease, and with much less than half the variations, maiming and distortion of the text, have reduced any common prose out of any language! How much more still to find in almost every line, words, and sometimes whole verses mutilated, stretched out or lopped off, transposed or exchanged ad libitum, in order to bring them to his ill contrived standard! To hear a learned prelate, with all the seeming gravity imaginable, affirm that the Hebrew poetry, (which by the way was arrived to such prodigious heights, with respect to the grandeur and loftiness of its figures and imagery, even so early as Mose's time) was even so low as in David's time, so crude, imperfect and vague, as not to have so much as a determinate difference between long and short syllables, especially considering to what a heighth of perfection that monarch had improved the art of music; and, what is still more surprising than all the rest, to see his lordship, in consequence of this his low conceit of the Hebrew poetry, take such pains to marr, deface, and destroy some of the most surprising, lofty and complicated figures and allusions in that sacred book, and such as far excel all that is to be met with in the Greek and Latin poets. But for these I must refer the reader to what I have observed of the Hebrew poetry, and on that absurd performance, in the Universal History (see vol. iv. of folio edition p. 710 & seq. and notes, and in the octavo one, vol. x. p. 202 & seq. and note (E). The occasion of my being obliged to make those animadversions on it, was as follows.

I was so shocked at the freedom which that prelate took to depreciate, mutilate and vilify so sublime a set of the noblest and most divine poems, that I thought myself obliged to write against

him, and to expose, as they deserved, all his unfair criticisms on
it, all his forced emendations, and, above all, the absurdity of his
new-discovered metre; but withal, in such a respectful manner,
as was due to a person of his character. And in order to that,
retired for three months into Surry and Hampshire, where I had
an opportunity to consult, upon proper occasions, some of my
friends, who were no strangers to that kind of learning. I found
the task the less difficult, as I presently fell in among some of
them, who not only condemned his performance, but had raised
already some very material objections against it, which they
readily communicated to me as soon as they were apprised of
my design. One of them among the rest had (by way of exposing
his lordship's contemptible metre) reduced the English Lord's
Prayer, Creed, Ten Commandments, and the Te Deum, into the
same crawling measure; whilst I, who wholly confined myself
to the Hebrew, had already done the same by the first chapter of
Genesis, and the last chapter of Malachi, both which I had likewise
turned into the same dull verse, without half the deviations from
the text, which his lordship had been forced to make in almost
every Psalm. Some of his very pretended emendations proved
such, that the frequency of them directed me to the discovery of
a more elegant metre than he had ever dreamed of, and which
convinced me, as they have since many more Hebraists, that
there was in the metre of the Psalms, not only a real and settled
distinction between the long and the short syllables, but that two
of the latter were equivalent, in the constituting of a foot or verse,
to one of the former; so that they had at least three different kinds
of feet, viz. long monosyllables, bisyllables, consisting of two
long, and trisyllables, consisting of two short and one long, or
vice versa; but which in the metre answered to a spondee, or
two long syllables. Of this I gave so many instances, as made
me think, contrary to what I had done till then, that the Hebrew

metre was not so irrecoverably lost as I had imagined, and that a little more application than I had time then, or have had since to bestow upon it, might go near to recover most, if not all, the various kinds of it.

However, as soon as I had finished what I, and some of my friends as well as I, thought a sufficient confutation of the bishop's performance, and in the same, tho' not so florid and elegant a Latin, I sent to desire one of my booksellers to enquire of Mr. Bowyer, whether the new types, cast for his lordship, were still in his possession? and whether I might be permitted the use of them, in the answer I had prepared for the press? I was answered in the affirmative; but one bookseller took it into his head to ask at the same time, what number of copies his lordship had caused to be printed of his Psalter? and was answered only five hundred; one half of which had been presented by his Lordship to his learned friends, both in and out of England, and most of the rest were still unsold, there being but few among the learned, that were curious in such matters; the performance having been disapproved by all that had seen it. This news so cooled the booksellers eagerness after my answer, that, upon my coming to town, and their acquainting me with the state of the case, I was quite discouraged from printing it. For they concluded from what Mr. Bowyer had said, that it would be dangerous to print above three hundred of mine, the charge of which being deducted, the profit, upon a supposition that they were all sold, would be so small, that they could not afford me above two or three guineas for my copy (which would have made about seven or eight sheets of a middling octavo) without being losers. This was their way of computing the matter, against which having nothing to object, I locked up the papers in my cabinet, where they have lain ever since. They did indeed offer me better terms, and to print a greater number of copies, if I would be at the trouble of printing it in English, which they thought would be more universally read, out of dislike to the bishop; but, besides that I cared not to be at the pains of Englishing it, I thought it below the subject to print it in any other language, but that in which his was wrote, and so wholly declined it.

I lodged then with the curate of the parish*, who, upon my coming from Hampshire, told me the following story, which I give on his authority, for I never enquired farther into it—That his rector, the reverend Dr. Nichols, acquainted the bishop, that he had a gentleman in his parish, who designed shortly to publish a confutation of his Hebrew metre. The bishop asked whether he was equal to the task? and was answered, that he was thought so by all that knew him, and that he was the person who had wrote the Jewish history, wherein he had given a greater character of the Hebrew poetry than his lordship seemed to do in his book, and that he was one of the persons concerned in the writing of the Universal History. The bishop then asked his name, and being told that he called himself Psalmanazar, expressed himself with some warmth to the company, that there was never a Jew of them all that understood any thing of Hebrew, much less of the sacred poetry; and being told that I was no Jew, but in all appearance an honest and strict churchman, who would doubtless use his lordship with the respect due to his character; he appeared a little better satisfied, and willing to suspend his judgment, till he saw what I had to say against him.

And here I cannot forbear making an observation, or two, on his lordship's speech, taking the story for true, which I am the more inclined to believe to be so, because he was always known to have a singular contempt of the Jews, so far as related to their knowledge of the Hebrew tongue. The one is, that his mean opinion of them must be owing to his small acquaintance with them; otherwise he might have found in London several of them very learned in that tongue, (besides a much greater number abroad, especially among the northern ones) and who, bating their different interpretations of those main prophecies which relate to the Messiah, could have displayed to him a much greater and deeper skill in that sacred tongue, than he appears to have had, by any thing one can find in his book. The other is, how his lordship came to take Salmanazar for a Jewish, instead of an Assyrian name; for as the monarch so called, was one of those monarchs who carried away part of Israel captives into Assyria; a Jew would as soon call a son of his Beelzebub, as Salmanazar, or Nabuchadnezzar.

However, the abovementioned story, as well as the expectation which my friends in Hampshire, Surry, and London, were in, to see my answer to him, gave me no small regret, lest my not publishing it should be interpreted in favour of his performance, or as my yielding the point to him, as not being able to confute him. And could I have afforded it, I would have run the hazard of printing it at my own charge; for I was above doing it by subscription, it being so small a thing as a pamphlet of at most eight octavo sheets; and much more loth was I, all the above things considered, to let a work seemingly calculated to depreciate the excellence of the sacred poetry of the Old Testament, to go uncensured; especially as I had so many strong objections ready levelled against it. At length a thought came into my mind, as I was then preparing new materials for the second part of the Jewish history, to resume that subject there. And this I thought, I was so much better intitled to do, if it were but in defence of what I had said in the first part in praise of the Hebrew poetry, and which was, in most cases, quite opposite to the character, which his lordship gave of it in his book. The collecting, and compleating of the canon of the sacred books by Ezra, and other inspired writers, and their appointing of the proper lessons, psalms, &c. for the divine worship, gave me a fair opportunity for it, which I was the more ready to take, as I knew that it would be read by many more people in such a work as that, than in a Latin pamphlet, and would of course more effectually expose the absurdity of his pretended new-found metre, as well as the unseemly freedom he hath given himself in altering and mutilating the sacred text for the sake of it. I therefore resolved to take notice, in justice to his lordship, of all just, laudable, and useful discoveries he had made on that subject in the text, and to throw the main part of my objections against the rest of his book in a long note, in the most succinct and impartial manner I could, in hopes that the setting both forth, as it were, in one view, might probably excite some who had more learning and leisure than I, to follow the hints there given, as the most likely means for compleating the desired discovery, to which his lordship had in a great measure opened the way, though he had so unhappily miscarried in the end. The difficulty was how to contract my materials so as not to over-swell that part of the work, as it must have done if I had brought every thing into it, which I had wrote on that subject, and this obliged me to strike off near two thirds of them, and to confine myself to the most material points, such as would most effectually answer the two main ends I had in view, viz. the exploding the bishop's new metre, and giving the curious reader, that would go about it, a clue to find out the original one of the sacred books; for as to what I designed to have said in praise of the Hebrew poetry, had the subject been printed separately, it was the less necessary here, as I had already expatiated so much upon it in the first volume. Some of the proprietors and authors were indeed against my design, not only as it would swell the chapter beyond its length, but likewise as the subject in question appeared to them, foreign to the rest of its contents; but I had the pleasure not only to carry my point against them, but likewise to have the performance commended by several learned men as well as by all my friends; insomuch that upon my consulting several of them, whether I might not in the second or octavo edition (in which we were obliged to contract our materials, in order to reduce the whole within the proposed limits) either wholly omit or content myself with a short mention of what I had done more at large in the folio; they advised me by no means to curtail the main subject, though I might, they thought, eraze here and there an explanatory or critical note, which I readily complied with.

Soon after I had concluded my last part of the Ancient History, the proprietors and authors had some meetings together to consult upon the going on with the Modern, and several plans were proposed by different persons of learning and capacity. The misfortune was, that this part likewise was to be confined within the compass of twenty volumes, of the same bulk with the Ancient, and these gentlemen differed so much in the proportion they allowed to each respective country or kingdom, that we could see but little likelihood of making any tolerable computation, either of what the whole might reasonably amount to, or of what number of sheets might be properly allowed to each history. As for me, the more I considered the great extent of the work, and the number of empires and kingdoms which had not so much as been touched upon in the Ancient part, such as Turkey, India, the great Mogul, Tartary, China, Japan, &c. the greatest part of Africa, and the whole tract of America, to say nothing of Russia and several other northern countries in Europe; the more I was persuaded of the impossibility of reducing the whole within so small a number of volumes, unless it was done rather by way of epitome, than of compleat, though ever so succinct, a history. But though this appeared still more visible by the small number of sheets which these plans, however different, allotted to most parts of the work, and must have received by almost every reader, at the first view, yet the proprietors who had their particular reasons for fixing upon that number of volumes, would by no means consent to have it exceeded. This however occasioned some demur, during which some of the best judges in this kingdom, and out of it, were consulted, as well as about the properest method of beginning and pursuing this modern part.

# About The Author

"George Psalmanazar" is assumed to have been born around 1679 in the south of France. He claimed to have been born in Formosa, and used the deception to get to Londion in 1704, where he was feted as an exotic Asian. His book on Formosa was a best-seller and for years many believed his story which he never fully denied during his lifetime. He died in 1763, in London after decades there as a writer.

Lightning Source UK Ltd.
Milton Keynes UK
UKHW042017150422
401613UK00001B/30